Table of Co 

The Art of Creative Thinking

Expand your creative problem-solving, logical thinking, and decision-making skills to propel yourself to the top of your field.

Sagar Chakraborty

Chapter 1: Introduction

****

"If you always do what you've always done, you'll always get what you've always got."
- Henry Ford

What This Book Can Do for You?

In the real world, there are, of course, so many examples of innovation and creative problem-solving that they could fill a whole book.

Yet, I am aware that that is not your sole desire. You're here because you want to learn the basics of using creative problem-solving and goal-setting techniques to improve your life. You want to know how to improve your brain power to improve your idea generation and solution-providing abilities.

This book will alter your view of your own creative abilities while removing the mystery surrounding the creative process. Your life's course can be dramatically altered by your ability to produce ideas that work.

Maybe you'll start to see a world of possibilities opening before you. It will teach you to:

- Come up with ideas whenever you need them.
- Locate alternative sources of revenue.
- Generate untapped commercial potential.
- Enhance the effectiveness of currently held beliefs by manipulating and adapting them.
- Launch brand-new items, offerings, and methods.
- Create approaches to difficult issues in the corporate world.
- Focus on the upside of challenges.
- Develop your capacity for output.
- Take the role of "idea person" in your team.
- Find out how to find the next big thing.

I want to teach you the most effective ways to come up with new ideas and new ways of thinking whenever you need them. I realize that is a bold assertion but hear me out.

Many of the most creative minds in the world use the techniques I describe in the book; they are not unique to me. As it has been effective for them, it ought to be effective for you and me (yep, I am on the same path). Everyone can benefit from learning to think creatively.

Don't assume that only a small number of people in the arts can come up with original ideas. As a side note, don't think that creative problem-solving is only for businesspeople with a lot of skills and global goals.

Don't limit yourself to a small niche or force yourself along a predictable road that will only lead to average outcomes. Anyone interested in deviating from the status quo would benefit from cultivating creative thought. Every successful person prioritises finding the best solutions with the least amount of effort and resources.

Let's now start with a story on creativity.

A Story of Creativity

A long time ago, a guy named John owned and operated a powerful industrial conglomerate. He realised one day that his company was lagging its competitors and wasn't as innovative as it once was. John acknowledged the inefficiency of using outdated ways of thinking and addressing problems. He was aware of the need to inspire his team members to think creatively.

John called a meeting of all employees and asked for suggestions for how the company could improve. He promised that the best idea would be put into action and that its creator would be compensated monetarily.

The staff took an interest in the mission and began brainstorming solutions. One of the engineers proposed the idea of using drones to transport goods between storage facilities. Another worker proposed a novel recycling programme with the potential to save costs and reduce trash. A housekeeper offered the most novel and resourceful suggestion, which was to reuse waste products to create new environmentally beneficial products.

John chose to take the housekeeper's excellent advice. The company has a new division that focuses on creating innovative recycled products. This not only reduced their trash and carbon footprint but also increased their profits.

As a result of this project's success, there is now an atmosphere of creativity and innovation throughout the company. John realised that encouraging employees to think creatively might lead to success and that the best ideas frequently come from unexpected sources. John has made it his mission ever since that fateful day to promote the free flow of ideas among his team members.

I learned about this in a book. It's not obvious to me if this is based on actual events. Whether or not the story is based on actual events, the lessons it teaches us are applicable whenever we consider the various directions our own lives could go.

When trying to solve an issue, do we merely consider the few obvious possibilities, or do we use our imagination and creativity to generate novel, unexpected solutions that help us move forward more quickly and effectively?

Most of the time, we don't challenge our assumptions, so our outlook on possible outcomes is the same as everyone else's. Therefore, everyone would adopt the same approach, and productivity would be about the same as usual.

Imagine for a second what it would be like if you had access to information and knowledge that the public missed. Wouldn't that completely change the way you make choices and lead to better results?

Obviously, this would make a huge difference in your self-esteem and, by extension, your happiness.

Before we go any further, let's examine some real-world scenarios in which a creative strategy impacted several businesses to better understand how creativity works. A l

Real world creative example

Let's use Taco Bell as an illustration.

Glen Bell (1923–2010), a native of Downey, founded the well-known American fast food chain Taco Bell in 1962. Taco Bell has taken some unorthodox approaches to developing and promoting new menu items. Doritos Locos Tacos are a perfect example of this concept being put into practise.

Doritos Locos Tacos have a unique taste and texture since they are encased in a Doritos chip shell. A client requested this item in 2009 via Taco Bell's Facebook page, and the company's marketing department obliged.

Unfortunately, the Doritos chips' flavour often rubbed off and made a mess when attempting to construct a taco shell. Taco Bell's R&D team worked with Doritos maker Frito-Lay to create a shell that could withstand being stuffed with taco fillings.

After their introduction in 2012, Doritos Locos Tacos quickly became a best-seller, with sales of over a billion servings in just the first year. In addition to giving Taco Bell customers something new and exciting to try, the product also helped set the company apart from its rivals and boost sales.

Taco Bell's success with the Doritos Locos Tacos has encouraged the chain to keep taking risks with its menu. Instances of this include the Naked Chicken Chalupa (a taco in a fried chicken shell) and the Cinnabon Delights (a dessert made with cinnamon rolls from Cinnabon). Taco Bell's willingness to explore new things, both in terms of ingredients and presentation, has helped it become a market leader and a household name among younger, more adventurous customers.

Let's take another example.

Lever was founded in 2015 and develops software. San Francisco, California, is home to the company that Sarah Nahm, Nate Smith, and Randal Truong started in 2012. Through its advanced applicant tracking system (ATS) and recruitment tools, Lever aids organisations in their search for, hiring of, and retention of top talent. As an example of its innovative thinking, Lever has adopted a "candidate-centric" strategy for hiring.

The founders of Lever, Sarah Nahm and Nate Smith, realised that candidates typically felt dissatisfied with the standard application and interview processes and that this might result in the loss of talented individuals and poor candidate experiences. Lever chose to take a new approach to hiring by focusing on providing a positive experience for job seekers, increasing the likelihood that they will choose to work for the company.

Lever accomplished this by including state-of-the-art functions, including flexible application forms so users can showcase their relevant expertise and talents, straightforward interview scheduling, and instantaneous candidate feedback. They made sure it was user-friendly and tailored to the candidate's abilities when creating the programme.

Lever has been successful in attracting and retaining top talent by setting itself apart from the competition and placing a premium on the application experience.

Lever's innovative approach has improved the application and hiring processes for candidates and helped the company's customers attract and retain top talent. The company's approach demonstrates how companies can improve their recruitment process and produce commercial success by focusing their efforts on the needs and experiences of job seekers.

Let's take one example from the sports world.

In 2002, the RiverDogs of Charleston, South Carolina, a minor league baseball team, came up with a novel strategy to increase ticket sales. The group agreed to have a "Nobody Night," during which spectators would not be admitted to the stadium.

Mike Veeck, the son of famed baseball owner Bill Veeck, is the team's marketing director, and he came up with the concept to raise interest and publicity. Despite selling tickets, the team did not allow fans inside the stadium. They were instead invited to a pregame party with food, drinks, and live music held away from the stadium.

Fans could view the game from the rooftop of an adjacent building or via a hole in the outfield fence. Outside the stadium, the team had a very large video display screen set up so that spectators could keep up with the action.

"Nobody Night" was a smashing success despite the offbeat theme. After their game sold out, the RiverDogs became the focus of national media attention. "Nobody Night" helped boost interest in the team, leading to a rise in attendance for the rest of the season.

After a "Silent Night" game in which supporters were asked not to make any noise, the RiverDogs hosted a "Salute to Professional Wrestling" event, rebranding themselves as the "Charleston Rainbows" and inviting professional wrestlers to take part in the game.

After seeing the effectiveness of these campaigns, other minor league baseball teams sought out Mike Veeck to help them increase attendance using similar methods. "Nobody Night" is still remembered as one of the most popular and successful promotions in the history of minor league baseball.

You can observe the rapid pace at which new technologies and innovations are being developed because of the widespread use of creative thinking. Just two generations ago, these kinds of innovative concepts would have seemed like something out of a science fiction novel.

It's mind-boggling to think that innovative thinkers like Elon Musk and Richard Branson have led to a shift in perspective from Earth as the centre of the universe to serious consideration of space travel and the establishment of space tourism. Ashton Kutcher, Leonardo DiCaprio, and Justin Bieber are just a few of the celebrities who have put down

$250,000 deposits to secure their spots on Richard Branson's spaceship, Unity Spacecraft.

It's amazing how many jobs a robot equipped with AI can handle nowadays. Take the example of ChatGPT.

ChatGPT is made for natural language processing (NLP) tasks like chatbots, systems that answer questions, and translating languages. It has been trained on a wide range of topics and can understand and create text in many different languages. This makes it a useful tool for many different uses.

As a language model, ChatGPT works by looking at the text you give it, figuring out its context and meaning, and coming up with a response that fits best with what you gave it. It does this by using a mix of algorithms for machine learning, such as deep learning and natural language processing.

Which of these stories deals with the subject? They illustrate how "the act of thinking outside the framework," or creative and innovative thinking, has contributed to the development of humanity.

Chapter 1 Introduction: Key Takeaways

If you think creatively, you can find more solutions to any problem, even if there only appear to be a few.

Anyone, whether an individual or a large corporation, can improve upon their current operations and point of view by taking a fresh look at the situation. The personal and organisational examples show how thinking creatively can lead to novel insights and fresh ways of perceiving the world.

Furthermore, creative problem solving is not restricted to a select group of artistically endowed people or reality-bending, world-changing business leaders. If one believes they can learn how to think creatively and is ready to put in the time and effort to do so, they will enhance their creative thinking abilities and discover unexpectedly new and unpredictable ways of addressing problems.

Every growth-oriented person **who wants to discover and direct their life in ways they couldn't have imagined before** will find useful information and guidance in this book.

Chapter 2: How the Brain Works: A Tour of the Creative Hub

****

"The left brain has been popularly associated with logical thinking, while the right brain has been associated with creativity. This is an oversimplification."
~ Roger Sperry

Let's Have a Look Inside the Brain

Let's take a trip inside your brain and explore the architecture that allows you to think creatively and beyond the box; this will help us all understand the concept.

Prior to 1950, the left hemisphere of the brain—the side of the body that also contained the heart—was widely considered to be the most important component of the brain. Evidence pointing to the left hemisphere being responsible for language comprehension began to emerge in the early nineteenth century. As time progressed, the right cerebral hemisphere gained a reputation for being less developed and more reliant on instinct than its left counterpart. This led scientists to conclude that the left side of the brain was superior.

But it wasn't until 1950 that it was determined that the right brain is the superior part of the brain; this was done by Roger Sperry, who is famous for the split-brain research and won a Nobel Prize in medicine for his efforts. He said, "The so-called subordinate or minor hemisphere, which we had hitherto considered to be illiterate and mentally impaired and thought by some experts to be non-conscious, was found to be in fact the superior cerebral part when it came to executing certain sorts of mental work."

Sperry went on to say that the differences between the hemispheres represented two distinct ways of thinking. The left side of the brain was in charge of thinking in steps, analysing things, and managing language. Conversely, the right hemisphere of the brain was responsible for more abstract thought, pattern recognition, and reading people's feelings and body language.

Various Studies have shown that the left hemisphere has a more linear, systematic way of looking at the world, whereas the right hemisphere is more open-minded and intuitive in its approach to reality.

The study of split brains was a breakthrough in neuroscience; it shed light on how each hemisphere of the brain works and opened the door to investigations into brain lateralization and specialization.

Sperry won the Nobel Prize for this work, which changed how neuroscience and psychology looked at the mind and how it works on the inside. When Sperry died in 1994, the New York Times said that he "overturned the prevailing orthodoxy that the left hemisphere was the dominant part of our brains."

American art teacher and author Betty Edwards wrote a great book called "Drawing on the Right Side of the Brain" in 1979. It went into a lot more detail about how right-brain thinking works. She didn't agree with the idea that some people are just not creative. She thought that drawing wasn't that hard, but that the problem was how people saw it.

Edwards's work was partly based on what she knew about neuroscience, especially the research on the cerebral hemispheres, which showed that the two sides of the brain do different things. But instead of focusing on where the hemispheres are, she gave the modes the names "L-mode" and "R-mode." She said that L-mode thinking is mostly verbal, analytical, and sequential, while R-mode thinking is mostly visual, perceptual, and global.

In the last few decades, technology has helped us learn a lot about the brain. Not only did Robert Sperry come up with new ideas, but Betty Edwards popularized the idea of the right hemisphere. The invention of fMRI (function magnetic resonance imaging) made it possible for people to scan and think about how neurons in the brain move and work. fMRI showed the proof by showing how blood moved to different parts of the brain while they were doing different things.

For example, if you are doing a hard math problem, the scan would show that your blood is thick on the left side of your brain. On the other hand, when people did creative work, watched emotional movies, or just let their minds wander, the right hemisphere had more blood cells that gave the brain the energy it needed.

In a nutshell, the myth that the left hemisphere, or left brain, was better than the right brain was busted in the second half of the 20th century. It was decided that both parts of the brain play a big part in the different things that go on inside the brain.

Let's understand the Functions and types of thought processes handled by the left and right hemispheres of the brain and how they are distinct from one another. Key distinctions between the left and right hemispheres are as follows:

The left side of the brain is linked to analytical thinking, math skills, and logical reasoning. In contrast, the right hemisphere is responsible for things like imagination, creativity, and the ability to express oneself artistically.

The left hemisphere of the brain plays a more significant role in language processing than the right. Instead, the right hemisphere is responsible for interpreting nonverbal cues, including body language and facial emotions.

The left hemisphere of the brain is responsible for precise activities like reading, writing, and arithmetic, while the right hemisphere is more attuned to the big picture. On the other hand, the right hemisphere of the brain oversees more artistic and imaginative pursuits, as well as having a greater grasp of the broader picture.

The left hemisphere of the brain oversees logical processing and making logical decisions, whereas the right hemisphere handles intuitive processing and making intuitive choices.

The left brain is more prone to the sequential and linear processing of information, while the right brain is more likely to process information holistically, looking at the big picture rather than the details.

So far, we've talked about the left and right sides of the brain as if they were two separate functional units that you could turn on or off. But this is the wrong way to do it. When making decisions, both hemispheres can help each other out by looking at both the big picture and the small details.

Even though it was true that the left brain had been in charge of business for a long time, because most work in the industrial age (manual work done with industrial machines) and the information age (knowledge work done with technology) required people to use their logical and analytical skills, this meant that the left, logical side of the brain was used more.

But with the fast and consistent automation of knowledge work and the fast progress in the field of artificial intelligence, most of the work that only the left brain can do can be done by machines. According to a report, McRobots using artificial intelligence that operates 50 times faster and more accurately than humans are already operating McDonald's stores. This is because artificial intelligence works best when there is a clear process for doing things in a logical way.

Now that you know how both sides of the brain work in a broad sense, you also know that you can't just get by using your left brain (logical thinking) and ignoring your right brain (imaginative, creative thinking).

So, the next step is to think about how you can use what you've learned.

You must want to know how you use "creative mindset" to solve problems. I think you're more interested in learning tried-and-true methods that will help you think on your feet and come up with ideas whenever you want.

So, let's get right to the meat of the matter. From now on, we'll get into the "how-to's" with specific instructions so you can start using them in your everyday life.

Why is Box Compared to a Brain?

Information processing in the brain is frequently explained by comparing it to a box.

Like a box can only house so many things, so too can the human brain only handle so much data. The amount of mental work that needs to be done to finish a task is called its "cognitive load". When there is too much to think about, the brain can lose its ability to work properly.

Just as a box can be labelled to make it simpler to find specific goods, so too can one's brain be organized to facilitate quick access to specific bits of information. The cognitive functions responsible for this are paying attention, remembering, and learning.

Furthermore, the brain is divided into several areas that are each responsible for a certain task, much like a box can have separate sections for storing different kinds of objects.

So, the concept of information processing in the brain, as well as the various ways in which the brain is organized and functions, may be better grasped through the lens of the brain being like a box.

Quantity: Since the box has four walls and no open space at the top or bottom, it can only hold a finite number of objects. If a box can only hold 40 items, you obviously can't store 100 packages in it. There's a limit on how much you can keep in there.

Type of Contents: The contents of the box will be uniformly varied in type, with some fluctuation due to the size of the items you place in it.

You wouldn't risk placing heavyweight steel things inside a box that was made specifically to store and take the weight of a set number of cookie packets, would you? In the same way, the types of things that can be placed inside the box are restricted.

Most individuals, unfortunately, treat their heads like file cabinets. Let's work on our comprehension.

The unintentional (but frequently potent) influences of our families, schools, communities, and religions have an impact on our minds from the time we are young until we are financially independent.

We mislead ourselves into thinking that our choices matter. Unfortunately, the involuntary imprints of our environments frequently misdirect our "so-called conscious" decisions. Years or decades of social conditioning have a profound effect on an individual's belief system, which in turn influences most of their decisions, both little and large.

Unfortunately, unless someone decides to raise their level of consciousness by exposing themselves to a different environment and choosing to think beyond the effect of conditioned thinking, this becomes a programmed pattern for most of us. Hence, the quality and amount of content in our mind (i.e., our thoughts and creativity) become constrained only by the extent of the design (conditioning) of our mind's box.

A person with a narrow or sheltered worldview is often referred to as a "frog in the well" because of this common metaphor. The frog in this metaphor has spent its entire life in a well, and as a result, it can only understand its immediate surroundings.

This metaphor can be used in the study of human behaviour to show that people who aren't exposed to a lot of different cultures, ideas, and experiences may find it harder to understand and appreciate how rich and different the world around them is. It can also be used to inspire people to go out and learn about the world for themselves, meet new people, and gain a broader perspective.

Taken as a whole, the metaphor of the frog in the well shows how important it is to learn about and interact with the world outside of one's immediate sphere of influence.

In a similar manner, if you are born and raised in a household where the emphasis is on experiencing new things and taking risks, you will view life as an exciting trip.

But if you come from a more traditional and risk-averse background, you probably won't be able to think creatively until you actively seek it out or are exposed to a different environment.

When it comes to your thoughts, where do you now stand in terms of creativity?

You'll learn the history of the phrase "Creative mind" as well as the results of a fun activity that has been used to assess people's creative abilities for decades.

Where did creativity come from?

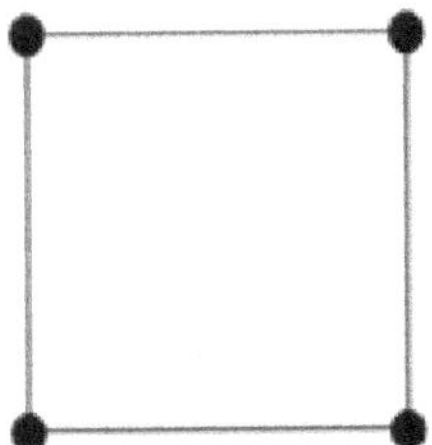

The four points in the image above define a quadrant, which is a rectangle with four equal sides and four right angles.

The four points in the image above define a quadrant, which is a rectangle with four equal sides and four right angles.

The goal is to increase the size of the quadrant by doubling it, and you may do this by repositioning just two of the dots.

If you have solved the four points problem above, let's take another problem.

The 9-dot puzzle is another creative problem-solving exercise in which players are tasked with drawing four straight lines to join nine dots in a 3x3 grid.

The solution to this puzzle lies in questioning conventional wisdom and pushing the boundaries of what you believe is feasible. Connecting the dots in a non-trivial way can help you locate an answer that wasn't there before. Solving this puzzle will force you to get out of your comfort zone and think beyond the box or obvious.

You have one go at connecting all these 9 dots without retracing your steps or putting down your pencil.

Relax for a second and use your brain to figure out what to do. Don't bother reading this any further unless you've already tried to solve the problem.

Okay, I'm guessing you've finished the drill and have returned. The correct response is provided at the conclusion of this section.

If you're like most individuals who have tried to solve this puzzle, you probably started out by drawing lines inside the imaginary square. Nevertheless, you won't find the solution inside such a box. To find the right answer, you need to draw lines that go beyond the confines of the box or square you've created in your mind.

This 9-dot puzzle is a great example of the idea that "Creative thinking" means going beyond the obvious and giving unconventional solutions a shot. that to come up with novel and superior solutions to challenges, one must be able to think creatively and beyond the obvious.

The 9-dot puzzle, often called the "Einstein puzzle" or the "Nine Dots Problem," first appeared in the public sphere rather than in print. It's a time-honoured challenge that's been deployed in a variety of settings to foster critical thinking and problem-solving. Connect nine dots in a square pattern using only four straight lines without putting down your implement of choice. Although the puzzle's provenance is murky, it's widely held that early 20th-century psychologist and philosopher Karl Duncker employed it in his study of how people approach problems. Throughout the second half of the 20th century, the puzzle gained popularity and is currently utilized in many different sectors to foster original thought and problem solving.

Because of this, the slogan "Creative mind" came to be used frequently by management consultants and executive trainers and is now considered a cliché.

Okay, I'm guessing you've finished the drill and have returned. The correct response is provided at the conclusion of this section.

Why Limiting Yourself Prevents You from Expanding

Most people never break out of their "cage" of conditioned thought patterns. Large organizations sometimes fell prey to the pitfalls of "inside the box" thinking, which ultimately led to their demise. In the corporate sector, there is no shortage of examples of "creative thinking outside the box or obvious" thinking becoming a failure. First, let's look at some of them and see how they stack up against creative thinking outside the box or obvious.

It is possible to stifle development by limiting our thoughts to what we already know, or "staying within the box," which might make us blind to new possibilities and answers. When we only come up with ideas that fit with our current paradigm, we limit our ability to think creatively and grow.

Some of the ways in which conventional thinking stunts development are listed below.

reduces the likelihood of coming up with original ideas and approaches to challenges by focusing on what is already known or experienced.

If we don't try to think outside the box or obvious, we might not find new ways to investigate problems or new ways to solve them.

Putting too much emphasis on what has been successful in the past can stifle creativity and cause us to miss out on potential areas for improvement.

How Thinking Inside the Box kills Growth

Companies that "thought inside the box" or were reluctant to change or adopt new ideas often saw stagnant growth. The following are some examples:

Kodak Once the undisputed king of photography, Kodak fell on hard times when it couldn't make the transition to digital. Kodak went out of business because it didn't adapt to the rise of digital photography and kept putting its focus on film-based products.

Take example of The Blockbuster video rental chain. They did very well in the 1990s and early 2000s, but when the market changed, they couldn't keep up. In the end, Blockbuster went bankrupt due to competition from online streaming services like Netflix and the declining popularity of physical media.

Once a dominant player in the retail industry, Sears fell on hard times as it failed to respond to the rise of e-commerce and shifts in customer tastes. The company's decline can be traced back to its insistence on having a physical presence in local communities and its reluctance to take advantage of the benefits of online shopping.

These instances show how a "stuck in a rut" mentality and a lack of flexibility can stifle development and success, even for established businesses. When it comes to fostering growth and success, an organization's willingness to accept and adapt to new ideas, technology, and consumer preferences is crucial.

Above, we see how conventional thinkers and creative thinkers approach problems in completely different ways.

Yet, here is the problem.

Most people have the false impression that only a small percentage of the population can think creatively. They believe that some people's brains are wired in a special way that allows them to think in unconventional ways, while the rest of us are limited to imagining just what we can see. Science and technology have shown that we all have the neural equipment for creative problem-solving.

Let's move on to the next chapter, where you'll learn how to build your inner infrastructure and a solid base for creative thinking.

Annexure: The solutions to the nine-dot problem and Quadrant challenge

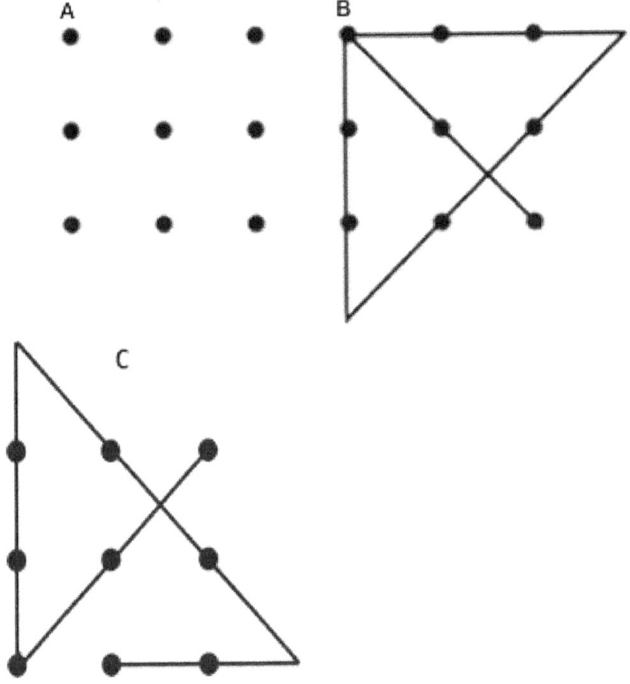

A – Problem, B -Solution1, C-Solution 2

The solution to the Quadrant challenge

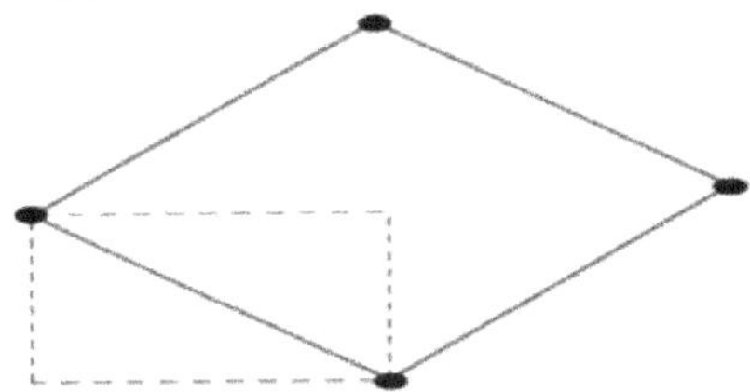

You can think of your mind as a box. The box can only hold a certain number of things, and only certain kinds of things can be put in each box. In the same way, our minds tend to think in the same way all the time. This way of thinking is usually limited and controlled by the kinds of thoughts that are fed into our brains unconsciously from the time we are young until we are adults with our own lives. Because of this, the **human mind can only think in a certain way that has been taught to it**.

The 9-dot exercise and Quadrant challenge help you figure out how you think, whether you use the traditional creative method or think outside the box to come up with new ways to solve problems. The only way to think differently and creatively is to get into creative mindset and see all the options around you, which you wouldn't be able to see if you only thought inside the box.

Before science could learn more about the brain, which didn't happen until the middle of the 20th century, **people thought that the left side of the brain was the smarter one** and that the right side was for retarded dreamers who didn't have anything to do with the real world.

Thanks to Robert Sperry, who won the Nobel Prize for his research, for showing the world that **the right side of the brain is very important** because it helps us understand the outside world in a broader context. Later, Betty Edwards's book "Drawing from the Right Side of the Brain" and the development of fMRI in neuroscience provided clear evidence that both sides of the brain work.

The left brain oversees the right side of the body, and vice versa, and each of the brain's hemispheres is responsible for a unique set of functions. On the left is a sequential process, whereas on the right is an instantaneous one. The left hemisphere analyses the written word, while the right considers the larger picture. The left hemisphere's strength is in analysis, whereas the right hemisphere's is in creative synthesis.

Chapter2: Key Takeaways

For much of human history, up until the middle of the twentieth century, **the conventional wisdom held that the left hemisphere of the brain is the more evolved and useful of the two**, while the right hemisphere is home to hopelessly unrealistic ideas that have no place in the real world.

The work of Nobel laureate and neurologist Robert Sperry has shown **how the right hemisphere of the brain is crucial for seeing the big picture** and understanding the world around us. Later, Betty Edwards's book "Drawing from the Right Side of the Brain" and the development of fMRI in neuroscience provided unmistakable confirmation of the symmetry between the two hemispheres.

The left side of the brain controls the right side of the body, and the right side of the brain controls the left side of the body. The left is sequential, and the right is simultaneous. The left side of the brain looks at the words, while the right side looks at the bigger picture. The left brain looks at things in a logical way, while the right brain puts things together.

The way you think is like a box. Both the number of objects and the kinds of items that can be stored in each box are limited. Similarly, we have a habit of thinking in a certain way on a consistent basis. This way of thinking is typically restricted and governed by the kinds of ideas that are instilled in us from early childhood all the way through adulthood. **The result is that we can only think in the limited ways that our conditioning has taught us.**

The Quadrant challenge and 9-dot exercise are useful tool for evaluating your thought process, whether you tend to stick to tried-and-true methods or seek novel approaches when faced with a challenge. The only way to think creatively and generate original ideas is to leave the safety of the familiar and explore the infinite possibilities beyond.

Chapter 3: Constructing an Internal Framework for Creative Problem Solving

****

"Believe in yourself and all that you are. Know that there is something inside you that is greater than any obstacle."
\- Christian D. Larson

Why Your Belief Is Crucial

We have often seen A person's beliefs shape their perspective, their behaviour, and their entire existence. How we see the world, our capabilities, and our potential all come from the ideas we have. They allow us to make sense of the world and the events that occur within it.

When we have faith in who we are and what we can do, we are more willing to take chances and work hard toward our goals. On the other hand, when we have self-doubt, we tend to pull back and play it safe, so restricting our growth and development.

The bonds we have with others are profoundly impacted by the convictions we hold. It's been shown that individuals and events tend to mirror our own internal beliefs, thus it's important to keep a positive outlook on life. On the flip side, unhealthy relationships and unfavourable experiences are often the result of holding negative views.

At the end of the day, our beliefs are a potent force that can shape the world around us. With the right mindset, we may attract happiness, success, and fulfilment into our lives. As our beliefs shape our actions and the world we perceive, they are, indeed, extremely important.

One real-life example of self-belief is Oprah Winfrey, a media mogul, talk show host, actress, and philanthropist; she is also a role model for having confidence in oneself. Oprah has never doubted her own worth or ability, despite overcoming poverty, violence, and tragedy in her childhood. She is widely considered to be one of the most successful and powerful personalities in the entertainment industry, despite having to overcome countless challenges and failures along the way.

It could have been easy for Oprah's early career setback when she was fired from her job as a TV news anchor to derail her aspirations. But she didn't let that defeat her; instead, she utilized it to switch gears professionally and follow her dream of being a talk show host. She had the confidence to start her own talk show, "The Oprah Winfrey Show," which became a smash hit and ran for 25 years, during which time she received several honours and awards.

Throughout her career, Oprah has always had a good opinion of herself and faith in her own abilities. She has used her fame to fight for things like equal rights for women, feminism, and social justice. She has been honest about her struggles with obesity, insecurity, and other problems, but she has always kept a positive attitude and worked hard to get better.

Oprah has demonstrated the power of self-belief in allowing us to succeed in our endeavours, follow our dreams, and make a difference in the world.

Just what are We supposed to take out from this?

Simple. If you don't have belief, you won't be able to take any action.

There is a spiralling upward relationship between one's level of conviction, the scale of one's acts, and the magnitude of one's outcomes. Better outcomes reinforce convictions, which in turn motivate you to work harder.

Let's talk about the 1980 United States men's Olympic hockey team, widely known as the "Miracle on Ice," is one sports story that illustrates the power of great confidence.

Even before the games began, the United States Olympic team was considered to have a strong chance of winning any medals, let alone the gold. They were largely college students competing as amateurs against professional teams from all around the world, notably the Soviet Union, which had won the gold medal in each of the previous four Olympics.

Yet the American squad was confident in its own abilities and felt it could hold its own against the best teams in the world. Coach Herb Brooks led by example, teaching his team the value of hard work and cooperation.

Most people thought the U.S. team would lose to the Soviet Union in the semi-finals. The score was close throughout, but the United States side managed to pull out a 4-3 win thanks to a pair of third-period goals. When the team won, it was seen as one of the biggest surprises in sports history.

After defeating Finland in the championship game, the United States squad took home the trophy. It was a victory that proved everything was possible with enough hard work, persistence, and faith in one's own abilities.

The story of the 1980 US Olympic hockey team has become an iconic sports moment because it has taught players everywhere to believe in themselves and their skills even when things seem impossible.

You came here to learn how to improve your capacity for original thought, so I know you're wondering why I'm spending so much time talking about stories.

There's a good explanation for it. Please have a look at the chapter's heading. The focus of this chapter is on laying the groundwork for creative thought from the inside. A firm conviction in your own ability to think creatively is essential before proceeding in this direction.

How the Power of Belief Can Boost Your Creativity

There is a lot of evidence to support the idea that a person's level of optimism directly affects their level of creativity. Studies have shown that the degree to which we think we are creative has a big effect on how creative we really are.

According to studies, those who view creativity as a learned competency are more likely to seek out creative outlets and come up with original concepts. Those who think creativity is something some people have, and others don't could be less likely to pursue creative pursuits or reach their full creative potential.

What's more, we may not be able to get past creative roadblocks and difficulties if we hold false notions about the nature of creativity, according to research. Persevere in the face of adversity and think creatively to solve issues; these traits are more common in people who view creativity as a process involving trial and error and learning from failures.

The converse is true for people who think creativity is a static trait: they may be less resilient in the face of adversity since they believe they aren't naturally gifted.

When it comes to creative projects, it's important to believe in the power of your own creativity, which shows how important it is to have a growth mindset. When we have faith in our own creative abilities and realize that imagination is a skill that can be honed, we are able to reach our highest creative potential.

There was a study conducted at a major publishing company to find out why some people were creative, and others were not. The results of the study surprised everyone because, all other things being equal, there was only one factor that determined whether a person would be creative or not: their personality.

The results were that those who thought they were creative were, and those who didn't think they were creative were not. Seems surprisingly simple but profound, isn't it? Let's watch what happens next.

The next step was for the company to set up training for the "so-called uncreative" (people who called themselves that) to give them effective ways to boost their self-confidence. After training, the results were astonishing. They all suddenly began coming up with far more original answers and suggestions than the first group of creative people, all of whom were convinced of their own creativity.

That's the impact of a confident outlook.

Those who are creative don't let their minds be influenced by pessimistic ideas. They are aware that negative thinking leads to stressful emotions like fear, worry, tension, depression, etc., and that once your mind is flooded with negative feelings, you are unable to think clearly and have no room to contemplate anything but bad thoughts.

Those who fall into the creative category always have a bright outlook on life. Optimism regarding potential outcomes is important to their mindset.

Let's take example of Nick Vujicic, an Australian-American evangelist and motivational speaker, is an inspiring example of the power of optimistic thinking. Nick was born with a rare genetic illness that left him without arms or legs. This presented him with several problems and difficulties throughout his life.

Nick was able to maintain a positive outlook and self-confidence despite his handicap. Rather than letting his impairment stop him, he decided to concentrate on his many positive qualities. He trained his feet to perform tasks that are normally performed by the hands, such as typing, writing, and even sports.

Nick has started speaking to audiences all over the world to spread his message of optimism and resilience. He's published a few books, including one called "Life Without Limits," which is all about helping people push above their own limitations and live their best lives.

Nick's success is a direct result of his optimistic outlook and self-assurance; he has motivated many people to follow in his footsteps. His life is a striking example of how persistence and confidence in one's own abilities can help people overcome seemingly insurmountable problems and lead to great successes and growth.

Our history is filled with innovative people who did not let pessimistic thinking stand in the way of their success because they focused on what was rather than what was not. Some people had it far tougher and suffered humiliation numerous times for failing to meet their targets, but they never gave in to discouragement.

- Can you imagine Thomas Edison giving up after failing his electric bulb experiment 500 times and crying in a corner of his room?

- Can you imagine Albert Einstein going to a remote, isolated location and discarding all his research notes because he was too busy and dissatisfied with the results? That sounds absurd, doesn't it?

- Do you possibly think it's possible to imagine someone as successful and inventive as Richard Branson or Elon Musk experiencing sadness and worry if one of their key initiatives fails miserably?

I believe you got the point. Those who are creative have confidence in their ability to produce something, and this confidence motivates them to work consistently on their projects.

Any path to success starts within you. As a result, strengthening your conviction that everybody and everyone can think creatively is the first step.

Challenges: How to Build Beliefs in Creativity

Let's be honest. When we feel good about ourselves and our abilities, i.e., when we believe in ourselves, we deal with life's challenges in a much more positive and upbeat way.

Everyone wants to believe in themselves, but few people do. What makes it hard?

There are three main problems that make it hard for us to build and strengthen our beliefs about good things. Michael Michalko, an author and expert on creative thinking, calls them FUDs, which stand for fear, uncertainty, and doubt.

1. **Fear:** You're afraid of failing, what other people will think of you, wasting your time, and other things. Fear shows you an imagined future that you want to avoid at all costs, so the obvious choice is to keep things the same. This keeps you from acting and getting results, and ironically, it makes your negative beliefs even stronger.

2. **Uncertainty:** The human mind likes to feel safe and know what will happen in our lives. They don't like not knowing what will happen in the future, unless it's a good kind of uncertainty that we call novelty. Any doubt about our safety in the future makes us feel anxious, which shakes our faith.

3. **Doubt:** We don't believe we're good enough to do something important. Even when we have some success, we sometimes still doubt our skills and give all the credit to luck instead of our own hard work. When we have doubts, we get imposter syndrome, which makes us feel like we don't deserve to be successful and makes us afraid that the world will find out we are a fraud.

When we have FUDs, our brains make a chemical called cortisol, which is a stress chemical and is linked to bad moods. This chemical makes it hard for us to think straight because it makes us feel bad.

This makes us act in a way that isn't helpful, so we can't do anything to change things and get results.

Michalko urges people to recognize and get past these FUD barriers if they want to be as creative as they can be. He gives people different techniques and exercises to help them break out of their usual ways of thinking and come up with new ideas.

Under the influence of FUD, you can't possibly come up with new ideas. For creativity to happen, there needs to be a place in your brain where neurons can fire and connect with other neurons that have different ideas. This makes for different neural pathways. But the feelings that these FUDs cause fill up all the space, making it impossible for new ideas to come up.

I'm not saying that you should ignore your fears completely and just keep going. We should be aware of these FUDs and not believe them. But instead of letting them make us feel bad, we should focus on doing things that will give us the power to eventually get rid of these bad feelings.

There are other difficulties too to consider besides FUD when trying to boost confidence in one's creative abilities. Some other major obstacles are as follows:

1. Limited Resources: Being creative often necessitates these things. When people's access to resources is limited, they may be unable to fully pursue their creative interests or experiment with new ideas. Finding new ways to solve this problem, such as forming partnerships or campaigning for more funding and investment in the arts, may be necessary.

2.External Validation: Beliefs in one's own creative abilities can be weakened by our culture's reliance on external validation, such as the pursuit of praise from others. Those who put too much stock in the opinions of others may lose confidence in their own originality and instead try to live up to the standards set by those around them. Overcoming this obstacle can be aided by encouraging people to have faith in their own judgement, recognise the importance of intrinsic drive, and prioritise their own development and satisfaction.

3.Time Constraints: Constraints on the Available Time might be challenging. To find time in a busy schedule to engage in creative experimentation. Time alone for contemplation, experimentation, and incubation is a common condition for productive creative thinking. It might be difficult to prioritise and set aside time for creative endeavours while still meeting other obligations, but doing so is crucial.

4.Resistance to Change: Creative problem solving typically entails rejecting conventional wisdom in favour of novel alternatives. But aversion to change can be a major barrier to strengthening confidence in one's ability to be creative. To conquer this obstacle, we must cultivate an environment that values creativity, recognises originality, and appreciates risk-taking.

5.Educational Systems: Standardised testing, repetitive learning, and uniformity are commonly emphasised in conventional educational institutions at the expense of encouraging individuality and originality. This can lead to a divide between classroom instruction and the cultivation of original thought. Addressing this issue can be aided by advocating for educational reforms that place a premium on creative thinking, critical thinking, problem solving, and multidisciplinary methods.

By being aware of and responding to these obstacles, individuals and groups can strengthen their convictions about the value of creativity and cultivate social and physical settings that encourage its expression.

Methods to Inspire Creativity

Now you know that you can't move a single step without faith. You also know how hard it can be to build a stronger belief, so what should you do next?

Now you need to find out how to change your beliefs in a powerful way.

Here are some ways to help people believe in their own creativity:

Encourage exploration: Tell people to try out different ideas and options without worrying about being judged or failing. This can help them learn to be open-minded and try new things.

Provide inspiration: Give people ideas by letting them see creative work in action and try it out for themselves. This can be done by showing them art, music, writing, and movies, among other creative things.

Emphasize the process over the product: Focus on the process, not just the result. Tell people to pay attention to the process of making something, not just the result. This can help them have an open mind and be willing to try new things.

Promote risk-taking: Encourage people to take risks and try new things, even if they don't know how things will turn out. This can help them believe in their own creativity and get over their fear of failing.

Practice positive self-talk: encourage people to talk to themselves in a positive way when they are trying to be creative. This can help them think in a more hopeful and growth-focused way.

Provide opportunities for collaboration: Encourage people to work together with other people. This can help them learn how to communicate, work as a team, and come up with new ideas.

Offer constructive feedback: Tell people what you think of their creative work in a constructive way. This can help them learn to have a growth mindset and see their mistakes as chances to learn and get better.

Foster a supportive environment: Make a place where creativity and new ideas can thrive. This can be done by giving people access to materials, tools, and technology, as well as by celebrating and recognizing the creative achievements of individuals.

Let's take example of Prescott Lecky.

Prescott Lecky, an American psychologist who helped start the field of self-image psychology, said that there are two powerful ways to change a person's worldview:

1. Confidence in one's own skills, **the realization that one has control over how he or she acts**, and the belief that one can do the tasks given to him or her well.

2. **It's the conviction that we're all as smart, creative, and capable as everyone else in the world**, and that we deserve to be always treated with respect and dignity.

This may seem like a restatement of what I've already said, but it's crucial that you grasp this concept on a deeper level. For an idea to stay in your mind for good, you must be exposed to it repeatedly.

Your mind will only believe that a good outcome is likely if you truly believe that you have the power to act and that you are just as capable and deserving as anyone else who has been successful. After determining what you want to do, it will provide steps to help you get there.

While the two powerful belief levers mentioned above are necessary for creative and original thought, fear, doubt, and uncertainty have the opposite effect. We need to take action to replace these FUDs with belief levers because they are incompatible with our minds.

Finally, Lecky understood that this was easier said than done. He understood the difficulty of eradicating ideas that had been lodged in our minds for years and even decades. Because your mind will present you with numerous arguments in favour of maintaining your current set of ideas, you will need to provide convincing evidence to support the replacement of your negative beliefs.

Self-affirmation

There is a fantastic method that can help you automatically internalize any belief. What I mean is to keep reinforcing these new beliefs until they become a part of who you are, a part of your identity.

Let's see if a metaphor can help us figure things out. There were audio CDs and cassette tapes for listening to music and other audio before the internet grabbed the globe by storm in the previous few years.

One useful thing about audio CDs and cassette tapes is that you can record new songs over the old ones, which erases the old songs and replaces them with new ones so you can listen to the new songs.

Our minds are no different. We are born without prior knowledge of any particular church, culture, or legal system. In another way, our minds were like empty tapes or CDs. But, as we got older, our parents, friends, society, and culture all began leaving lasting marks on our minds in the form of ideas and views. That's right; we've programmed the blank cassettes of our minds with the norms, values, and ethical assumptions of our culture. The only music in our heads would be the ones that other people had already recorded onto our minds' blank CDs or audiotapes.

Take the preceding example and add another instance. Let's pretend you meet the love of your life and end up marrying someone who practices a faith different from your own. And because you're committed to this person, you've adopted some of their religious tenets or practices. You and your significant other have decided to forego Sunday church services in favour of attending your partner's temple or other religious gatherings. This is a slight modification to previously recorded ideas in the form of newer ones.

So, here's the point:

Instead of leaving our views about how to achieve our most important objectives and dreams to chance, why not consciously imprint them?

Why don't we consciously decide to alter our thought processes by installing new neural pathways or behavioural patterns in the brain?

That can't be true, right?

The key is believing in one's own worth.

Let's be honest about the negative connotation that affirmations have before we go any further. Some critics argue that affirmations aren't effective since doing so is nothing more than giving in to a mystical, wishy-washy condition that has nothing to do with reality. It's true that I had my doubts regarding the power of the affirmations. I felt like I was making a complete fool of myself by believing and saying something that was obviously not true. The key is believing in one's own worth.

But my problem wasn't with the affirmations themselves; rather, it was with the way I was using them.

Most "self-help" authors will tell you to write your affirmations in the present tense, as if you already have whatever it is you want. It's easy to tell yourself things like "I'm living like a billionaire" when you're working a low-paying, unfulfilling job or "I have the best relationship with my spouse and children" when the truth is far different.

This kind of assertion has many issues.

Initially, you don't believe them because they don't seem real to you. Second, they give you a false belief in your worth and a brief sense of satisfaction before bringing you face to face with the harsh realities of life. Finally, they make it harder to reconcile your present circumstances with your future goal.

I heard about a more effective method of affirmation through several forms of affirmation statements from Hal Elrod's best-selling book, Miracle Morning.

Hal says that instead of telling yourself things that seem obviously false and dishonest, you should use affirmations that sound true and encourage you to act.

Saying something like "I'm already thin and fit currently" is not as effective as saying something like "I'm committed to reducing my weight by 15 pounds within 4 months, and therefore, I'm committed to taking all the necessary action, including workouts, diets, etc. that will bring me closer to my ultimate goal."

Create an affirmation like, "I am committed to believing in my creative talents and coming up with and writing down four new ideas every day that are related to my most important projects." This will help you stay motivated to think creatively and come up with new ideas on a regular basis.

Let me give you some illustrations of affirmative statements:

1. I deserve your admiration and affection.

2. My aspirations and objectives are within my reach.

3. No matter what difficulties may arise, I am confident in my capacity to overcome them.

4. I have faith in my own special set of skills.

5. I feel an overwhelming sense of gratitude for everything good in my life.

6. I deserve every bit of success and happiness that comes my way.

7. My limiting ideas and attitudes are ones I have decided to abandon.

8. I deserve to feel strong and healthy.

9. When I think about what I've accomplished and who I've become, I feel a sense of pride.

10. As far as I'm concerned, everything is unfolding perfectly for my greatest good.

It's crucial to find affirmation phrases that truly speak to you on a deep, emotional level. You can tell yourself about these things daily, write them down in a notebook, or post them somewhere you'll see them often, like a mirror or computer screen, to reinforce your positive thinking. By regularly reinforcing positive beliefs about oneself, a person can develop a more positive view of himself or herself and a more positive attitude.

Here are some self-affirmation statements by top authors:

1. "I am not afraid of storms, for I am learning how to sail my ship." Louisa May Alcott
2. "I am enough just as I am." Brené Brown
3. "I am the master of my fate; I am the captain of my soul." William Ernest Henley
4. "I am not what happened to me; I am what I choose to become." Carl Jung
5. "I am not a product of my circumstances. I am a product of my decisions." Stephen Covey
6. "I am capable of achieving anything I set my mind to." Tony Robbins
7. "I am worthy of love and respect, and I treat myself accordingly." Deepak Chopra
8. "I am grateful for all the experiences that have shaped me into the person I am today." Eckhart Tolle
9. "I trust in my ability to overcome any obstacle and emerge stronger than before." Elizabeth Gilbert

10. "I am confident in my unique talents and abilities, and I use them to make a positive impact on the world." Paulo Coelho

These affirmation statements can serve as a source of inspiration and motivation, helping people tap into their inner strength and resilience. By focusing on positive self-talk and beliefs, people can develop a more positive self-image and mindset, which can lead to more confidence, happiness, and success.

You should focus more on your accomplishments than your mistakes.

Changing one's perspective to place more value on successes than failures isn't easy, but it's doable with diligence and exercise. If you want to give your successes more attention, consider the following suggestions:

Do yourself a favour and keep a thankfulness diary, where you can record your daily appreciation for the good in your life. Looking on the bright side can help you see things in a more optimistic light.

When you accomplish something or reach a milestone, reward yourself by taking a moment to pause and reflect on your hard work. Just doing something you enjoy or telling a loved one about your accomplishment will do the trick.

Instead of wallowing in self-pity over past failures, try to see them for what they really are: learning experiences. Think about what you've gone through and how you can use that to your advantage moving forward.

Positive self-talk is a technique whereby you encourage and inspire yourself instead of criticizing yourself for your flaws. Focus on what you can do rather than what you can't by reminding yourself of your abilities, accomplishments, and positive attributes.

Put yourself in the company of upbeat and encouraging people who will cheer you on and encourage you to realize your potential rather than focusing on your flaws. As a result, you might feel more hopeful and want to think about the good things in your life.

You can feel better about yourself and have a more positive outlook on life if you remember your successes and look at your failures in a different way. If you put in the time and effort, this method of thinking can become second nature and propel you to even greater success.

Remembering the skills, traits, and actions you took that led to your past successes could help you do the same things again. Believe in yourself and your skills by keeping up the traits and actions that have helped you succeed in the past. These will help you feel better about yourself and more confident in your own abilities.

Remembering setbacks without trying to learn from them lowers confidence and dampens the will to pursue future ambitions.

Think about a period when you had an idea when others were still struggling with a comparable situation; this will help you develop your capacity to think creatively and come up with novel solutions. It might be a time in your life when you were able to express your creativity, whether that was in the classroom, on the job, or with your family.

Some people may think they've never had a mind-blowing thought strike them out of the blue, but they'd be wrong. Every one of us has participated in group brainstorming sessions where our contributions were valued. It could be a suggestion for a cost-effective family vacation, or it could be a suggestion for an improvement to how you do things at work that would result in big savings for your employer.

I suppose you can recollect at least a couple such instances if you take a break from reading and close your eyes for a moment to reflect on them.

Remembering good things from the past sends good signals to the brain, making it more likely that you will be able to do the same things in the present and future.

How to Put Everything together to Think creatively

When someone says they can think creatively, they mean they can think outside the framework and come up with new ideas. Some suggestions to help you think beyond the framework are as follows:

The first step is to formulate a precise problem statement. Start by articulating the issue or difficulty you're attempting to address. Keeping to this plan will help you concentrate and block out distractions.

Collect data and viewpoints: Talk to as many individuals as possible, from a wide range of backgrounds, to get as many different points of view as possible. As a result, you may be able to better grasp the issue at hand and come up with novel solutions.

Question preconceived notions: Be aware of any biases or preconceived notions that may be limiting your thinking and actively work to dispel them. Think about the reasons for established procedures and be open to new ideas.

You may quickly come up with many ideas using brainstorming techniques. As they can often lead to breakthroughs and inventive solutions, wild, unorthodox, and even seemingly unattainable ideas should be encouraged.

Test out your ideas and different strategies and see what works best. Try new things, and don't be afraid to change course if something isn't working. Try different approaches and iterate on them until you find one that works.

Have an open mind, listen to others' input, consider alternative viewpoints, and don't become dogmatic about a single solution. Maintain a state of fluidity and adaptability and be open to making course corrections.

By integrating these methods, you may train your brain to think in new ways and generate original approaches to solving problems.

Several online studies have found that the average person comes up with between 50,000 and 60,000 ideas every day. Nevertheless, it's fascinating to consider that more than 95 percent of those thoughts are repetitive in nature.

If you keep having unhelpful thoughts, this is a serious problem. Our current situation is the direct product of our habitual ways of thinking; we can never change our circumstances by taking any measures other than altering our thought patterns. It has been said by the Buddha that we materialize our thoughts.

Most of our brain's processing power is used by our automatic thinking, which happens without us having to think about it. The mind's purpose is to keep you alive, so naturally it prefers that you avoid thinking about anything novel or out of the ordinary. This, of course, leads to the strange situation where people tend to think about the worst-case scenario more than the best-case scenario.

The longer you've been running this old program in your head through mental repetition, the harder it will be to rewrite the software's coding (unless you are deeply committed to changing it). On the other hand, you can start the process of reprogramming your mind if you deliberately and knowingly select helpful concepts and confirm them aloud or silently in your head on a regular basis.

If you want to be able to think of novel answers to problems, you'll need to retrain the parts of your brain that have been led to believe that you were never meant to think creatively.

The affirmation could be something like, "I am dedicated to strengthening my belief that I am capable of thinking creatively most of the time and will take all the actions that strengthen my belief about my thinking abilities." This is a plausible vision of the future, and it should motivate you to devote yourself to performing the work necessary to generate original concepts.

Go out of the house and become involved in a group or network online where you can make connections with others far along the path you aspire to follow.

Chapter 3 Key Takeaways

The first step is to have faith. If you don't have faith in yourself and your abilities, you won't act in ways that reflect those beliefs. No faith, no hope, no change. Strong conviction >> huge actions >> greater outcomes >> even stronger convictions is the formula.

Fear, uncertainty, and doubt (FUDs) are the three main obstacles to creating a strong belief, and as long as they are in your thoughts, you won't believe that you can think creatively and provide creative responses.

You need to strengthen not one but two key beliefs. (1) that you can carry out your assigned duties; (2) that you possess the same inherent skills as anyone else.

If you want to change your worldview, **using self-affirmations in the form of "commitment"** will get you there faster.

Spend as little time as possible with negative people and maximise your time with those who inspire confidence in you.

Focusing on your accomplishments rather than your setbacks will help you move forward positively.

Chapter 4: Set Difficult Goals and Establish Habits to Begin Thinking Creatively

****

"Challenges are what make life interesting and overcoming them is what makes life meaningful."

- Joshua J. Marine

In the last chapter, we talked about how important it is to build an inner foundation by learning how to strengthen our beliefs.

Yet, a difficulty lies ahead. It's impossible to maintain our constant excitement about life. We're balancing good and negative thoughts, and they're often at odds with one another.

Everyone has felt both joy and sorrow at some point in their lives. According to psychological theory, these feelings exist on a spectrum, with positive emotions like joy and negative emotions like depression at opposite ends of the spectrum.

Both positive and negative emotions have been proven to have profound effects on one's psychological and physiological well-being. Feeling good emotionally, especially joy, can boost your health and happiness. On the other hand, negative emotions, such as sadness, have been linked to unfavourable effects on mental and physical health, such as increased stress and the chance of developing chronic diseases.

Sadness, like joy, is a normal and natural human emotion and a part of everyone's life. Expecting or attempting to deny the existence of unpleasant feelings, such as sadness, is also neither healthy nor reasonable.

One of the main goals of human psychology is to study and improve ways to manage and direct one's emotions. You can do this by asking for help from family, friends, or trained mental health professionals. You can also try things like cognitive restructuring, mindfulness meditation, and changing your behaviour.

Human psychology is important because of the impact that one's ability to recognize and control negative and positive emotions has on one's health and happiness. Using healthy coping mechanisms can help people face the ups and downs of life with more composure and grit.

As a result, it appears that we could all benefit from a stimulus that encourages the kind of action that opens the door to new ideas. We should also schedule our daily activities so that we can use our imaginations frequently.

Daily Routines to Promote Creativity Everyday

Having a daily routine can help you build the habits and ways of thinking you need to live a creative life. A daily routine can help you become more creative over time by giving you structure, teaching you discipline, giving you time to think, reducing decision fatigue, and giving you a sense of community.

In this section, we will discuss practices that are well-researched and scientifically proven to enhance creative thinking.

Exercise is crucial for maintaining both physical and mental health. Consistent physical activity can enhance cardiovascular health, increase muscle strength and flexibility, raise mood and energy, and reduce the risk of chronic diseases such as obesity, diabetes, and heart disease.

To reap the benefits of regular exercise, it is recommended to engage in at least 150 minutes of aerobic activity each week at a moderate intensity or 75 minutes of aerobic exercise at a robust intensity. Also, it is recommended that at least two days per week be dedicated to strength training to grow muscle and improve general physical function.

There are numerous methods to incorporate physical activity into daily activities, such as walking or biking to work, using the stairs instead of the elevator, or joining a fitness class or sports team. To maintain consistency and long-term adherence, it is essential to select physical activities that are fun and sustainable.

So, regular exercise is an important part of a healthy lifestyle and should be a top priority if you want to stay in good health.

Regular exercise has been found to increase the production of brain-derived neurotrophic factor (BDNF), which can improve cognitive performance, mood, and executive function. It can also stimulate the production of other neurotransmitters, such as dopamine and serotonin, which can improve mood and reduce stress.

Several researchers have helped us learn more about BDNF and how it affects the health and function of the brain. These are a few prominent researchers and their BDNF-related studies:

Eric Kandel is a neurologist who has done a lot of research on the molecular basis of memory. He won the Nobel Prize for this work. BDNF is a key part of making memories, and he and his colleagues found that increasing BDNF levels can help people learn and remember more.

Michael Merzenich is a neuroscientist who has studied how experience changes the way the brain works. His study has demonstrated that BDNF is involved in the process of brain plasticity and that boosting BDNF levels may improve the brain's adaptability to new experiences.

Carl Cotman is a neuroscientist who has investigated how exercise affects the health and function of the brain. His research shows that exercise can increase the amount of BDNF in the brain, which may help explain how exercise improves memory and mood.

Along with many others, these researchers have helped us learn a lot about BDNF and how it helps the brain work and stay healthy.

Researchers from the University of California, Irvine, conducted a randomized controlled experiment. Male adults were randomly assigned to either an aerobic exercise group or a sedentary lifestyle group for the study.

After six weeks, BDNF levels went up by 32% in the group that did aerobic exercise, but they went down by 14% in the group that didn't do much. Increased BDNF levels in the exercise group were related to enhanced cognitive performance, particularly in the areas of attention and memory.

This study provides additional evidence that exercise, BDNF, and cognitive performance are linked. Regular aerobic exercise appears to enhance BDNF levels in the brain, which may contribute to the cognitive benefits of exercise.

Several studies have indicated that strength training can enhance BDNF levels in the brain. In a 2018 study published in the Journal of Strength and Conditioning Research, a single session of strength training was found to enhance BDNF levels in young adult men.

In 2016, the Journal of Sports Science and Medicine published another study that showed that young, healthy women's BDNF levels went up after eight weeks of strength training. Increased BDNF was associated with enhanced cognitive function, particularly in the areas of attention and memory.

These results suggest that strength training may be a good way to increase the amount of BDNF in the brain and improve cognitive performance.

Another research carried out by Stanford University researchers have found that walking is beneficial for physical and mental health, including improved mood, creativity, and cognitive function, as well as a decreased risk of chronic diseases. Walking for at least 30 minutes per day is linked to increased brain connections and enhanced cognitive function.

Several Leaders and executives have adopted the practice of having meetings while walking, such as Steve Jobs, Mark Zuckerberg, Jack Dorsey, and Barack Obama. These meetings can help stimulate creative thinking, improve decision-making, and provide a more relaxed and casual atmosphere for discussion.

Generation of ideas to promote creativity

Getting ideas can help people be more creative, grow, solve problems better, feel more confident, get more motivated, and do better in their careers.

Research has found that people are more likely to have creative ideas when they are performing activities like walking, taking shower, swimming than when they are sitting. Walking increases blood flow to the brain, and swimming improves the mood and reduces the symptoms of depression in participants. Swimming promotes relaxation and reduces stress, which improves creative thinking and problem-solving skills. Additionally, taking breaks helps to re-energize the mind and can result in the generation of novel and creative thoughts.

Let's take few examples.

Taking a shower makes you more creative and gives you new ideas. In the shower, people have come up with many great business ideas, products, and entertainment ideas, such as the idea for Virgin Atlantic Airways, the hit TV show Breaking Bad, and the famous Beatles song "Yesterday." When we let our minds wander and get rid of distractions, we can tap into our creative potential and come up with new ideas. Archimedes ran out naked from a shower, saying "Eureka," after he found the solution to the problem he had been searching for weeks.

Do you know the reason.

The phenomenon of experiencing sudden creative insights while taking a shower has been the subject of scientific study. Research suggests that the sensory stimulation, relaxation, and altered cognitive processing that occur during showering may all contribute to enhanced creativity. Some of these are relaxation, less stress, more dopamine, a break from conscious thought, and more connections between ideas.

Alice Flaherty is a neurologist and neuroscientist who has conducted extensive research on creativity. She has found that creativity is associated with increased activity in the prefrontal cortex and certain types of mental disorders. She has also explored the role of dopamine in creativity, suggesting that it may be involved in the experience of "flow" that creative individuals often report. Showers have been found to increase dopamine levels in the brain, which can facilitate creative insights by allowing the brain to make new connections between ideas. Research suggests that sensory stimulation, relaxation, and altered cognitive processing may all contribute to enhanced creativity.

Taking a daily shower has been found to promote relaxation, reduce stress, and increase dopamine levels in the brain, which can lead to enhanced creativity and idea generation. The sensory stimulation of taking a shower can help to engage the brain and promote relaxation and mental clarity, making it easier to think creatively and generate new ideas. Taking a shower can also give people a short break from the stress of daily life and help them clear their minds so they can think more positively and optimistically.

Walking is also a powerful tool for promoting idea generation, as it increases blood flow, reduces stress, exposes us to nature, encourages movement and change of scenery, and provides uninterrupted time for thinking and reflection. It also helps to clear the mind and improve our ability to generate new ideas.

Do you know the reason.

Studies have found that physical activity like walking can increase dopamine release, leading to feelings of pleasure and reward. Dopamine receptors in the brain can be increased by regular exercise, which makes physical activity more rewarding and enjoyable. This can make people more likely to keep exercising and improve their overall health and well-being.

Dopamine release in the brain is associated with the joy and reward of physical activity, according to research published in the journal "Neuron" in 2008. Dopamine production in the brain's reward centres was shown to be highest when the exercise was most gratifying, as measured by PET scans of the participants while they were engaged in physical activity. Acquire more of dopamine to invite creativity through this simple practice.

Mindfulness meditation helps in creativity.

Many studies have connected mindfulness meditation to a variety of cognitive and psychological benefits that can boost creativity. Below are some information regarding the relationship between these advantages and creativity:

Mindfulness meditation can help you focus on the task at hand, which is important for coming up with creative ideas and finishing creative projects.

Attention, empathy, and self-reflection: Mindfulness meditation can help you pay more attention and be more aware, so you can stay involved in the creative process and learn more about your own thoughts and feelings. This increased empathy and ability to think things through can also help you connect with your audience or target market and come up with ideas that will resonate with them.

Memory improvement: Mindfulness meditation can help you remember creative ideas, strategies, and processes by making your memory and recall stronger.

Mindfulness meditation can promote learning by increasing attention and focus, decreasing stress and anxiety, and fostering a more optimistic outlook. This can help you learn new creative skills, ways of doing things, and ideas that you can use at work.

Mindfulness meditation can boost creativity by making it easier to concentrate, focus, be aware, remember things, and learn new things.

The two most prevalent styles of meditation are focused attention and open monitoring.

Focused attention meditation: For this type of meditation, you focus on a single thing, like your breath or a mantra. When your mind wanders, you simply return your focus to the subject at hand. This style of meditation is frequently employed to enhance concentration and decrease distraction.

Open monitoring meditation: During open monitoring meditation, you observe your thoughts and emotions without judging them. You merely observe them as they arise and let them pass without attaching yourself to them. This style of meditation is frequently used to develop present-moment awareness and acceptance.

Both methods of mindfulness meditation are advantageous for creative thought. But open monitoring meditation may be especially effective for inventive thinking since it can help you create a non-judgmental and receptive attitude toward your own thoughts and experiences. This allows you to investigate and accept numerous options without being constrained by prior preconceptions or biases, which can help you produce fresh ideas and perspectives.

In 2012, Lorenza Colzato and her colleagues did a study to find out how open monitoring meditation and creativity, especially divergent thinking, are related. Participants in the first experiment were randomly assigned to either an open monitoring meditation group or a control group. After the meditation or relaxation session, all participants completed a creativity task that measured divergent thinking, and the results showed that participants in the open monitoring group generated significantly more original ideas on the creativity task compared to the control group. In the second experiment, researchers looked at whether the effects of open monitoring meditation on divergent thinking were caused by changes in cognitive flexibility. Cognitive flexibility is the ability to switch between different mental tasks or points of view. The results showed that open monitoring meditation performed significantly better on the cognitive flexibility task than the focused attention meditation and control groups.

In another study, Fadel Zeidan and colleagues investigated the relationship between open monitoring meditation and divergent thinking in 2010. When it came to the creativity task, the people in the open monitoring meditation group came up with a lot more unique answers than the people in the focused attention meditation group.

This suggests that open monitoring in meditation enhances divergent thinking and creativity. One important thing that came out of the above studies was that high observation scores were the only reliable way to predict creativity. This ability, which is boosted through open-monitoring meditation, not only improves working memory but also increases cognitive flexibility and decreases cognitive stiffness, all of which are essential to the creative process.

How to perform Open-Monitoring Meditation?

How do I perform open-monitoring meditation?

John M. DeCastro, author of the Contemplative Studies blog, describes open monitoring mindfulness meditation in a manner that is both comprehensive and self-explanatory.

This passage will assist you in beginning open-monitoring meditation.

Here is how to commence:

"When we do open monitoring mindfulness meditation, we open our minds to everything we feel, no matter where it comes from."

We continue to focus on the sensations associated with breathing, but we broaden our focus to include all bodily sensations, such as the feelings of touch, coldness, or heat from the skin; the pressure exerted by gravity on our rear ends while sitting on the chair or cushion; tingling sensations on the skin and elsewhere; sensations from muscles and joints; the subtle feeling of our heart beating with the ensuing blood pressure surges; and the subtle feeling of our lungs expanding and contracting.

In addition, we pay attention to exterior stimuli, including sights, sounds, tastes, and scents. Even with our eyes closed, we can sense visual stimulation, some of which is the result of light piercing the eyelids and some of which is the result of spontaneous activity in the brain systems underlying vision. In open monitoring meditation, we allow everything into our awareness and do not attempt to concentrate on or reject anything.

The openness of the mind includes the heart. Although we do not actively engage in thought, it nonetheless occurs. In open monitoring meditation, we make no attempt to prevent them. We simply observe them increasing and declining."

You should incorporate open monitoring into your everyday schedule. But, if you engage in open monitoring mindfulness meditation prior to beginning your most critical tasks, it will prime your mind and connect everything entering your subconscious mind, allowing you to develop additional ideas.

Monitor your distracting habits.

Checking social media or email frequently

Checking social media or email frequently can have negative effects on a person's well-being and productivity, such as decreased productivity, increased stress, poor time management, disruption of sleep patterns, decreased face-to-face interactions, and an increased risk of depression, anxiety, and other mental health problems. It is important to be mindful of the time spent on social media or email and to set healthy boundaries to avoid the negative effects.

Researchers have found that checking social media or email too often can hurt productivity, stress levels, time management, sleep patterns, and mental health. One study found that switching between tasks a lot can cause people to be 40% less productive, feel more stressed, have trouble keeping track of time, have trouble sleeping, and feel more alone. Based on these results, it seems that checking social media or email too much can hurt productivity, stress levels, time management, sleep, and mental health.

Dr. Twenge is a social psychologist who has done a lot of research on how technology affects the mental health of young people. In her book "iGen," she talks about how the rise of smartphones and social media has made it more common for teens and young adults to feel anxious, sad, and alone.

Dr. Rosen is a psychologist who has studied the impact of technology on cognitive processes and behaviour. His research has shown that checking social media and email often can make people less focused, less productive, and more stressed.

To avoid these harmful effects of social media and email, it is essential to engage in appropriate technology usage. This may involve establishing parameters for social media and email use, such as limiting the amount of time spent on these platforms daily, avoiding checking social media or email before bed or immediately upon awakening, and disabling notifications for non-urgent communications.

Some possible treatments I apply in my daily life will help you relax, like yoga or meditation, spending time in nature, and talking to friends and family in person. It is also important to know when using social media or email is bad for your mental health and to get help from a mental health professional.

Watching too much TV

When you watch too much TV, it can hurt your work, your physical health, your mental health, your social life, and your exposure to dangerous information. It is crucial to be careful with the amount of time spent and to prioritize other essential tasks.

Several studies have found that excessive television viewing has negative effects on physical and mental health, academic performance, and the ability to think. To improve overall health, it is important to limit time spent in front of a screen and do other healthy activities.

Researcher Dr. Herbert found that television advertising stimulated a significant increase in brainwave activity in viewers, particularly in the alpha and theta frequencies. His research had implications for the advertising industry and contributed to a growing body of evidence suggesting that television viewing can have a powerful impact on viewers' cognitive and emotional states.

Researcher Mihaly Csikszentmihalyi is a psychologist known for his work on flow and the effects of television on people's well-being. He argues that excessive television viewing can lead to boredom, apathy, and dissatisfaction, and suggests that people need to find activities that challenge and stimulate them to experience a sense of fulfilment and well-being.

You can't make connections between different ideas if you're always watching TV, using your phone, or doing something else that takes your attention away.

Your mind requires distance and/or rest. If you are continually connected to distractions, it will be far more difficult for your brain to rest and form associations.

You should either be creating or regenerating. This is how you should plan your day. Don't get me wrong. I am not opposed to relaxing after lengthy work hours. You need time to refresh and re-energize your mind to begin another productive day, but binge-watching Netflix or television for hours is not the ideal approach to refreshing. You can read a work of fiction or limit your television viewing to 30 minutes every day (but be careful not to let yourself glued to the TV for hours once you get started).

To lessen the bad effects of watching too much TV, it is important to use media in a responsible way. This could mean putting a limit on how much time is spent watching TV, getting up and moving during commercials or after watching TV, and choosing shows with positive themes and values.

You could hang out with family and friends, read books, or do other intellectually challenging things, or get professional help if watching TV is hurting your mental health.

Spending excessive time discussing rumours or personal matters

Negative outcomes may result from engaging in gossip or discussing private matters, including but not limited to lost time and productivity; strained relationships; a damaged reputation; elevated stress and anxiety; difficulty concentrating; being easily distracted; having one's words misunderstood; and moral dilemmas. To keep oneself happy and productive, one must regularly participate in deep conversations, work on one's own development, and cultivate relationships based on mutual trust, respect, and empathy.

Research has shown that excessive time spent discussing rumours or personal matters can have negative impacts on relationships, productivity, social comparison, self-esteem, emotional impact, and perceptions of trustworthiness and credibility. Gossiping can lead to negative perceptions of the person involved, decreased productivity, social comparison and self-esteem, emotional impact, and perceptions of trustworthiness and credibility. However, the specific effects of excessive time spent discussing rumours or personal matters may vary depending on the context and individuals involved.

Research by Kurland and Pelled (2000) has shown that engaging in gossip or discussing personal matters can lead to negative perceptions of the person involved. Gossiping can erode trust, strain relationships, and create a hostile or toxic social environment.

In another study by Duffy and Sedikides (2001), engaging in gossip or personal discussions may involve comparing oneself to others or participating in judgmental conversations. Research suggests that these behaviours can contribute to decreased self-esteem and feelings of inadequacy.

To sum it up the most important details for avoiding rumours are to be self-aware, communicate effectively, set the tone for courteous discourse and prudence, switch gears when gossip comes up, actively listen, don't be a part of the rumour mill, seek for people who value constructive dialogue, foster an atmosphere where people feel secure and supported, and consider the consequences of gossiping. It is important to uphold values and encourage a positive community, and the benefits to relationships and well-being are worth the time and work it takes to quit the habit.

How do we put everything together?

I did not intend to overload you with several habits and rituals that make it tough for you to even get started. So, I only chose the methods that will help you come up with creative solutions to your most pressing problems right away.

You can easily incorporate the above routines into your daily life without compromising your existing obligations.

I think it would be easy for you to add more showers to your routine on top of your morning shower. If you already take two to three showers every day, that's fantastic, and you may already be experiencing a dopamine rush in your brain. Exercise is necessary for physical health and disease prevention, so why not use it to boost our creativity as well? The mind is the source of all inventive thought; thus, employing a few mindfulness practices provides the best return on your time investment, so it makes perfect sense.

I do all these things regularly, and I've noticed a change in the way I think creatively and come up with new ideas. I hope you will begin incorporating these practices into your daily life and witness the magic for yourself.

How do we make such triggers?

Creating something new gives our brain something to do that it enjoys.

Let's now talk about the advantages of setting a challenge and how to start one.

Set a challenge to encourage creative thinking

Select a Specific Challenge

Convincing your mind that you have a specific problem to solve is far more satisfying than simply trying to think creatively without a defined goal.

Consider the following scenario: You won't be inspired to drive your bike faster unless you know where you're going and when you're going to get there. Your mind would understand the challenge if you specified the destination and the time required to get there. It will now be continually aligned with the final goal of driving quicker to arrive at the destination on time.

Likewise, our minds do not fully activate unless we present it with a specific issue to handle. Let's go over how to recognize the type of difficulty and how to communicate it to our minds in three easy steps:

Step 1: **Identify the exact Issue.**

Unlike most people, original thinkers don't view challenges as something to be avoided at all costs. Issues, in their view, are simply opportunities in disguise. For them, difficulties present an opening to make the most of the situation. Since you are interested in reading a book about winning mindset, you probably aren't afraid to try new things.

Your problem should be about something you care a lot about and solving it should help you get a long way toward your goals.

Without genuine motivation, your mind won't be able to stay stuck on the issue for as long as it takes to find a solution.

So, figure out what the issue is (In that process identify your opportunity).

Step 2: The following step is to break down the problem into **specific challenges.**

Let me illustrate this with an example. Imagine you wish to double your product or service sales in the next six months; this is the identification of the problem.

By asking precise questions like:

-What are the numerous platforms or channels that you need to use to improve sales?

- Do you need to approach someone for assistance or partnership to increase your sales?

-Does the approval of someone in authority increase your chances of success?

You can include as many questions as you want about finding a solution to your situation.

These questions will present you with a series of problems for your mind to solve. When you have a clear set of questions and know that the answers to those questions will help you solve the problem, your mind will see those questions as problems that need to be solved.

If you're seeking a fresh opportunity, here is the place to be.

The people of the world have a lot on their minds. The process of developing ideas begins here.

Step 3: The final but most critical stage is to **give your mind convincing reasons** for coming up with an idea. Make a list of the benefits and rewards, whether financial, emotional, or otherwise, that you wish to accomplish by solving the problem before you decide to solve it.

What are the immediate advantages? It could be money, market recognition, your brand, or anything else.

Does it help you live a better lifestyle by saving you time and effort in some way?

Do you have opportunities to collaborate with others in your sector, which offers you indirect access to other business opportunities?

What are the indirect benefits? It could be the gain of new skills, information, more freedom to spend time doing activities you enjoy, and so on.

How would you feel emotionally if you found a solution to your problems?

To emphasize, your mind will be more likely to come up with new ideas when the benefits and rewards are clear and important to you.

Take a break from reading now.

Think about your unique and important problem, break it down into specific problems by asking questions, and imagine what it will be like to solve the problem.

Perform this exercise for 10 to 15 minutes in a focused and distraction-free environment. You'll receive first-hand experience, and I'm convinced you'll come away with a slew of new ideas.

So, let's move on to the next point, which will help you find answers to your problems in a variety of places.

Creativity is stimulated by exposure to experiences.

When we do everyday tasks, our brains use neural pathways that have been set up by the repeated firing of the same type of neurons. These connections between neurons make it easier for the brain to do something with less effort and save energy.

Learning is the process of building and strengthening brain connections through repeated firing of neurons. This is how people can do things automatically and without thinking about it. By using already-established neural connections, the brain is able to do routine tasks with less energy. This lets it put its resources toward thinking processes that require more concentration.

The brain is an organ that needs a lot of energy, and it is always trying to save energy while doing all its important jobs. By relying on already-established neural pathways for normal tasks, the brain can save energy for other important tasks like consolidating memories, staying focused, and making decisions.

But using known neural pathways is helpful for normal tasks, but it can make it harder for the brain to adapt to new situations or learn new skills. The brain is hardwired to use the same neural pathways repeatedly. This makes it harder to create new ones when faced with new problems. This is why it is essential to continue learning and be exposed to new experiences, since this can aid in the development of new brain connections and promote neural plasticity.

In the end, creativity is nothing more than the capacity to produce fresh, unique, and useful work.

Also, according to one study, "openness to experience" was seen as one of the most constant attributes of creative ability when assessing a person's creative ability.

Openness to experience has also been linked to a greater ability to deal with ambiguity and uncertainty, which are often necessary for creative problem-solving. People who are more receptive to new experiences are also more likely to seek out various information and perspectives, which can facilitate the generation of more unique ideas.

Overall, creativity is a complicated and varied idea, but research shows that being open to new experiences is a major factor that could help people come up with creative and original ideas.

How Sensitivity to Diverse Activities Can Enhance Neuroplasticity and, Consequently, Your Cognitive Abilities.

The objective of neuroplasticity is to depart from the prevailing regular pattern.

Diverse activities can aid in enhancing neuroplasticity and cognitive capacities. Here are a few instances:

Getting new skills: Learning a new skill, like how to play an instrument, speak a new language, or play a new sport, can help stimulate the brain and make new neural connections.

Researchers have found that regular physical activity increases neuroplasticity by increasing the production of neurotrophic factors, which help neurons stay alive and grow.

Meditation: When you meditate or practice mindfulness, your brain's structure, and function change. This makes it easier to focus, pay attention, and remember things.

Interaction with others: Participating in social activities and maintaining strong social connections can improve neuroplasticity and cognitive function.

Trying new things, like traveling to new places or eating foods from other countries, can help stimulate the brain and promote neuroplasticity.

Engaging in a variety of activities that challenge and stimulate the brain can aid in boosting neuroplasticity and cognitive ability.

According to Jhon Ratey, associate clinical professor of psychiatry at Harvard Medical School, "The brain is a dynamic organ, constantly adapting to the world around us. By engaging in activities that challenge us, we can enhance our cognitive abilities and promote neuroplasticity."[1]

According to John Medina, director of the Brain Centre for Applied Learning Research at, "Our brain is like a muscle, and just like any muscle, it grows stronger with use. The more we challenge our brain with new experiences and learning, the more we enhance its neuroplasticity and cognitive capacities. "Thus, anything that takes you out of your normal routine can boost your creativity and help you come up with new ideas.

Now, let's move on to the most-anticipated sections of this book, where I'll explain the most successful methods for generating ideas on

---

1.   https://www.bing.com/ck/

a?!&&p=1c7e9b8134449113eJmltdHM9MTY3OTQ0MzIwMCZpZ3VpZD0wZjQwNjAzN

C0yN2M1LTY3NGItMDkxOS03MWFiMjY2ODY2NzQmaW5zaWQ9NTY0OA&ptn=3&

hsh=3&fclid=0f406034-27c5-674b-0919-

71ab26686674&psq=John+Ratey&u=a1aHR0cHM6Ly9lbi53aWtpcGVkaWEub3JnL3dpa2kv

Sm9obl9SYXRleQ&ntb=1

demand. I'll see you in the next chapter, where I'll discuss excellent methods for generating ideas on demand.

Chapter 4: Key Takeaways

Science has shown that playing an instrument can help you become more creative. To generate more ideas on autopilot, it may be most helpful to establish a small number of routines.

Memory and creativity enhancing BDNF are enhanced by physical activity. Increase your BDNF levels by exercising vigorously.

The release of dopamine after a shower has been scientifically confirmed. Dopamine levels correlate with the likelihood of having novel thoughts. Thus, you should bathe more frequently.

Practise a form of meditation based on "open monitoring." You'll be able to observe more, including the inner workings of your body and organs, the sights, sounds, and smells of your surroundings, and your own mental processes. Your ability to think in novel ways will increase as you increase your capacity for observation.

Disconnect from social media and instead focus your attention on something you truly value. As

You need to broaden your perspective on life in general and embrace the specific challenge of coming up with ideas. Having more life experiences increases neuroplasticity, which in turn provides more opportunities for your brain to be creative.

As your mind wants to be sure of the **advantages of being creative**, it will develop more ideas in response to a specific and significant challenge than to merely sit and wait for ideas.

your mind wants to be sure of the advantages of being creative, it will develop more ideas in response to a specific and significant challenge than to merely sit and wait for ideas.Creative problem-solving strategiesYou need

Chapter 5 - Creative problem-solving strategies

****

"Creativity is seeing what everyone else has seen and thinking what no one else has thought."

- Albert Einstein

So far, you have discovered the process of designing your internal infrastructure and comprehended the importance of creating targeted challenges and establishing key routines to enhance your creative thinking abilities.

Now that you have established a suitable inner infrastructure and designed a conducive environment, it is time to dive into learning effective techniques for generating creative ideas more frequently.

So, Let's get started.

Embrace Boredom to Foster Idea Generation

Embracing boredom is a powerful way to open your creative flow. To do this, take a break from information and media, enjoy peace and quiet, schedule time for spontaneity, participate in mindfulness or meditation, and take part in low-stimulation pursuits. These practices can help you become more aware and present in your daily life, allowing inspiration to flow freely. Relaxation activities such as going for a walk, sitting outside, drawing, or doing housework can help induce a state of calm that is conducive to original thought. Free writing or keeping a journal can clear the mind of unnecessary thoughts and ideas.

Traveling to unfamiliar settings can open the mind to new possibilities and stimulate curiosity. Tolerance and acceptance of suffering can pave the way to new insights and innovations. Ex

Apple Inc.'s late co-founder, Steve Jobs, was famous for enjoying his share of boredom and isolation. He'd go on lengthy walks by himself or just sit and think. He found that his most insightful thoughts on product development and user experience came to him during these times of introspection and reflection. amples of branch es are:

Mark Zuckerberg, CEO and co-founder of Facebook, has spoken openly about his habit of taking periodic "think weeks." During these weeks, he withdraws from his normal routine and devotes himself to introspection. He deliberately isolates himself to foster creativity and plan for the future of his business. V

o society

Billionaire CEO and founder of Spanx Sara Blakely lives quite close to her office, yet she still gets up an hour early every day to drive around the city aimlessly. Spanx makes a wide range of slimming intimates, body shapers, hosiery, apparel, and more.

What is she thinking?

She explained in an interview that she finds her most creative moments to be spent behind the wheel, free from distractions (including her four children under the age of 10). Billionaire CEO founder of Spanx Sara Blakely lives quite close to her office,

Let's have a look at a few more illustrations:

While resting under a tree, Newton was unceremoniously presented with an apple. The law of gravity was born from his mind's random wanderings.

Google is well-known for its inventive culture, and the company has adopted several techniques to foster creativity and new ideas. The "20% time" policy is one such method; under this plan, workers are free to devote 20% of their time at the office to activities that aren't directly relevant to their jobs. Products like Gmail and Google Maps were created because of this policy, which encouraged employees to let their minds wander and experiment.

At Facebook, the culture promotes accepting boredom and using it as an opportunity for innovation. The "Hackathon" events are only one example of how the organization encourages its employees to pursue their own interests and try out new things in a safe environment. The "Like" button and Facebook Live are only two examples of what may be achieved with this method.

Amazon, famous for its focus on the client and its commitment to constant innovation, has adopted boredom as a means of encouraging creativity. Long-term thinking and questioning the status quo are two of the company's guiding principles for its leaders. Amazon values employees who take the time to engage in deep thought and meditation, cultivating an atmosphere conducive to the development of original concepts.

These businesses understand that boredom can be a source of inspiration and have instituted policies that encourage workers to pursue their own areas of expertise and ideas. These businesses have created a culture of innovation by allocating resources toward in-depth consideration and experimentation, and as a result, they have made great strides forward in their respective fields.

What do these situations have in common?

This demonstrates how some of our most brilliant insights are conceived when we allow our minds to wander freely and process whatever occurs to them. In other words, while you're bored, you come up with great ideas. early every day to drive around the city aimlessly. Spanx

Through their studies, neuroscientists and psychologists have learned a few things about boredom. Boredom causes the brain's default mode network (DMN) to become active, according to numerous studies. The DMN is linked to self-referential, daydreaming, and introspective thought. People are more active at DMN locations when they are bored.

Reality is our access to stimulation and pleasure has changed a lot because of modern technology, especially smartphones. But too much use can cause too much excitement and make it hard to pay attention. Smartphones have a lot of material, but some of it is meant to be watched or read without doing anything. This can make your mind tired and leave you without a sense of accomplishment. Smartphones and other modern technologies have changed the way we get information and entertainment, but how they make us feel when we're bored depends on who we are, how we use them, how engaged we are, and how much we passively consume versus how much we do. It's important to think about how people's personalities, hobbies, and tech use are different., body shapers,

I remember our childhood used to be characterized by strong family and community ties, exploration of the outdoors, hobbies and arts and crafts, and limited screen time. Technology has brought better access to information and communication, but knowing how childhood used to be can help understand how it affects children's lives.h

In today's digital age, we have the convenience of endless feeds and notifications on social media sites to keep us engaged and addicted. These notifications tempt us with messages like "You may like this also," "People also viewed this," and "recommended read inspired by your views," creating a continuous loop of content consumption. It is important to recognise the impact of technology on our lives and be mindful of our usage. It can lead to a sense of distraction, reduced productivity, and a constant need for stimulation, so it is important to balance digital engagement with other meaningful activities, set limits on screen time, and be aware of techniques used to keep us hooked.ery, apparel, and more.

To sum up, our brains are in an endless cycle of changing gears. Dr. Daniel Levitin, a neuroscientist, claims that switching your focus from one task to another sucks up brain nutrition since it forces the brain to perform a neurochemical switch. If you persist,

When you jump from one distraction to another, you exhaust your brain's glucose supply quickly. Glucose fuels your brain and gives you mental stamina. Research shows that each day, you only get so much willpower to work with. It's like starting the day with a fully charged, green smartphone battery. This battery drains during the day as you use your phone for calls, reading the news, checking social media, etc. By the time dusk rolls around, it's almost time for it to drain. The same thing happens to your energy if you constantly shift it between different activities.um up, our brains are in an endless cycle of changing gears. Dr.

According to research by Microsoft Corporation, the average human has a shorter attention span than the notoriously fickle goldfish (9 seconds).

The goal of developing social media and video platforms is to keep you constantly engaged with them.

Netflix popularised the phrase "Binge Watch." When asked about its rivals, Netflix has said that Facebook, YouTube, and sleep pose the greatest threats. Nut

Furthermore, codependency is no longer defined as an emotional dependence on other people.ince it forces the brain to perform a

Renowned American author Cal Newport's books and articles suggest ways to lessen one's reliance on their smartphone and foster more positive interactions with technological devices. He suggests adopting the philosophy of digital minimalism, disconnecting from digital tools for a set amount of time, encouraging "deep work," setting clear boundaries with technology, engaging in activities that are more in line with one's interests and values, and assessing and reducing the number of notifications they receive on their smartphones. Readers are encouraged to tailor Newport's concepts to their own needs and interests. The goal is to achieve a happy medium where people can get the benefits of technology without letting it take over their lives. neurochemical switch. If you persist,

Back in 2015, Manoush Zomorodi, author of Bored and Brilliant, challenged her audience to reduce their smartphone use and increase productivity and creativity. She asked them to delete apps and discouraged them from using social networking sites. One person admitted to feeling co-dependent on their phone. you jump from one distraction to another, you exhaust your brai

Think back on an ordinary day when you picked up the phone, perhaps to check the time, but instead spent forty minutes watching something else. You burst out laughing as you realised you had no idea why picked up the phone.

Is there any way out of this mess? Yo

Here are some ideas to help you predict and make the most of boring moments during the day:

Accept the boredom: boredom can be used as a time for introspection and mindfulness practise. Rather than picking up your phone or other quick distractions, try taking a deep breath, looking around you, and letting your mind wander. This has the potential to increase ingenuity, self-knowledge, and tranquilly.

Do Something Creative: Boredom is a terrific motivator for coming up with new ideas. Do something artistic like drawing, painting, writing, or playing an instrument during this period. Give your thoughts the freedom to wander and find an outlet here.

Get Some Reading In: Always have a book or e-reader on hand. When monotony sets in, curl up with a good book. Reading is beneficial in more ways than one; it may be both entertaining and educational.

Practise mindful observation: Take a conscious approach to monitoring your surroundings and see the world around you in a new light. Take in the sights, sounds, and sensations of your surroundings. This can be accomplished when idle at home, in a park, or in a queue. Using your senses can pique your interest and inspire gratitude.

Connect with Others: Make the most of your downtime by striking up conversations with those close to you. Just start talking to someone, whether they're a co-worker, friend, or complete stranger. Mental stimulation and relief from routine can be gained through engagement with others.

Move Your Body: When inactivity sets in, turn it into an opportunity to break a sweat. Take a stroll, do some yoga, or do a quick workout. Working up a sweat does more than just get your blood pumping; it also boosts your mood and general health.

Practise mindful daydreaming: Learn to daydream mindfully by letting your thoughts roam. Allow your mind to wander to fantastical places. This style of daydreaming has been shown to promote original thought and personal growth.

Keep in mind that boredom can be a helpful mental state that promotes relaxation, recharging, and the development of novel ideas. Accepting boredom and taking charge of your reaction to it can lead to the discovery of rewarding new perspectives, activities, and interests. ur brain and gives you mental stamina. Research shows that

Thus, you should welcome boredom so that a new mental space might arise, one in which ideas can develop, flourish, and eventually be appreciated. S

Nourish your mind extensively

Idea generation does not occur in isolation. There must be a foundation to build upon. As discussed in the previous section, the first step is to identify the problem and transform it into a well-defined challenge. By doing so, you narrow down your focus and determine the direction to pursue. However, merely defining the challenge does not initiate the idea generation process.

To generate ideas, it's important to do some groundwork. As you'll learn in this book, new ideas are often just combinations of existing ones. So, the first step is to enrich your mind with a diverse range of ideas. This is crucial because when these ideas interact with each other, they can generate novel and innovative solutions.

Creative thinkers understand the importance of constantly feeding their minds with new information and ideas, as they know that it is essential for their growth and development. As Dr. Seuss, a prolific author, mentions, "The more that you read, the more things you will know. The more that you learn, the more places you'll go."

Exposing your mind to diverse ideas is crucial, and often underrated. It requires an extensive amount of information to fuel the idea generation process. This is why there is a say that knowledge is power. By providing your mind with a diverse array of information, you equip it with the necessary ingredients to create a recipe for unique and original ideas.

Let's talk about some ideas to boost your mind while reading:

Take notes:

Taking notes while reading or studying improves memory and helps the brain strengthen connections between neurons, opening the door to creative problem-solving and new ideas.

Visualize the content:

Creating mental images of what you're reading has been shown to improve memory and promote neural connectivity in the brain. Making connections between what you read and what you already know can improve your comprehension and memory. Discussing what you've read with other people can help you learn more from what you're reading.

Read different genres:

Brain function can be enhanced, and neurons can be stimulated to form new connections and ideas through reading across a variety of genres. Reading works from a wide variety of genres forces readers to think critically about how they interpret the material they consume.

Reading fiction, for instance, can enhance our capacity for empathy and comprehension of complex social circumstances, while reading non-fiction, on the other hand, can broaden our horizons and deepen our awareness of the world. Poetry reading has been shown to foster more imaginative thought and a more profound appreciation of language.

Reading works from a variety of genres encourages the reader's brain to form novel associations between previously unrelated ideas. This is why we should always push ourselves to read something new and different from what we're used to.

Take breaks:

Taking periodic breaks during the workday has been shown to improve productivity and creativity. Taking breaks at planned intervals has been demonstrated to improve focus, productivity, and creativity. Changing your routine, going for a walk, or exercising are all good options.

Set goals:

By giving the mind something concrete to aim for, goal setting can boost cognitive performance. When we try to do anything, our brains go into overdrive, firing neurons and forming new associations to discover a method to make it happen. Since the brain is always trying to find new and better ways to reach the desired objective, this can lead to increased creativity and invention.

We are more likely to stay focused and engaged when we have a clear target in mind, both of which can be aided by defining goals. This can enhance our cognitive abilities and productivity by helping us focus our efforts where they will do the best.

Carefully choose the materials you intend to read:

Selecting reading content intelligently can boost brain function and create connections between neurons by exposing you to a variety of ideas and perspectives. The brain's ability to think creatively and solve problems is enhanced by being exposed to new ideas and information from a variety of sources.

You may motivate your brain to work harder and build new connections by reading stuff that is both tough and complex. Reading a book that requires you to think carefully and critically about a difficult subject, like neuroscience or economics, is one way to exercise your brain and boost your brainpower.

Read biographies:

By exposing the reader's mind to the perspectives of people from many walks of life and professions, biographies boost cognitive abilities. Reading about the trials and tribulations of others helps us learn from their experiences and develop our own creative solutions.

For instance, learning about a businessperson's tribulations and eventual triumphs can spark fresh ideas for a similar enterprise. Reading about an artist's creative process can inspire fresh ways of thinking about problems outside of art.

Read How-to books on a variety of subjects:

How-to books on a variety of subjects can increase cognitive performance and stimulate neural connections, allowing you to continually come up with novel ideas. Constantly challenging the brain to process and integrate new information through learning new abilities or refining current ones leads to the creation of new neural pathways and the strengthening of existing ones. This method is useful for enhancing intelligence, memory, and original thought. Reading how-to books has additional benefits, including the stimulation of creative thought and the development of novel insights since the reader is exposed to alternative points of view and methods of addressing problems.

Reading magazines and articles:

Magazines cover a wide range of topics, so reading them may be a terrific way to expand your horizons and spark inspiration. You may boost your cognitive talents and your ability to think creatively and solve problems by reading widely across a variety of topics and by reading articles that are both brief and easy to read.

Hiring people from other industries:

As a result of being exposed to new ideas, viewpoints, and methods of approaching problems, your brain's functioning can be enhanced by hiring people who have been successful in other fields. You can expand your knowledge, perspective, and approach to problems by collaborating with people from a wide range of experiences and perspectives. This can help you come up with novel ideas and connections you wouldn't have made otherwise. In addition, expanding your horizons by learning about other fields can reveal opportunities and approaches to challenges that you may have missed while working in your own.

Steve Jobs' 1983 appointment of John Sculley as Apple's CEO is often cited as an example of a successful cross-industry hire. Sculley, at the time Pepsi's CEO, was completely unfamiliar with the computer business. Jobs, though, saw Sculley's potential to inject Apple with new ideas and marketing know-how.

The Macintosh and Apple II were two of Apple's most successful products that were released during Sculley's tenure as CEO. However, they finally had a major disagreement, leading to Sculley firing Jobs.

Despite this, Sculley's accomplishments at Apple are still held up as a prime illustration of how appointing an outsider with specialized skills can boost a company's performance.

Attending business seminars:

Attending business-related seminars, conferences, or other events can be a fantastic way to pick the brains of successful people, expand your horizons, and spark creative thinking. Attending these kinds of gatherings allows one to learn more about their field, make connections with other experts and business owners, and observe emerging trends and advancements first-hand.

For instance, learning about the most up-to-date marketing techniques, tactics, and tools by attending a marketing conference Attending a seminar on entrepreneurship can teach one about the difficulties of starting a firm, strategies for dealing with them, and how to create a workable business plan.

Additionally, these gatherings provide an excellent opportunity to network with other attendees and industry leaders. They can learn a lot from these people and expand their network, which can aid their business.

Tony Robbins, a famous businessman and motivational speaker, is often cited as an example of someone who benefited from attending business conferences. Robbins is a regular at and speaker at business events like the Inc. 500 Conference, the CEO Summit, and the World Business Forum. Robbins has used the knowledge he obtained from these experiences to create prosperous enterprises and assist others in reaching their objectives by teaching them about leadership, personal growth, and business strategy.

Content Analysis:

To extract meaningful information from large amounts of raw data, content analysis is commonly used. You can learn more about the content and the author's intentions by employing content analysis. This can improve your cognitive abilities by:

Improve your critical thinking and analytical abilities by learning how to examine and understand data as part of a content analysis.

Analysing a wide range of content provides you with exposure to new viewpoints and ideas, which in turn might inspire you to solve problems in novel ways.

Gaining exposure to new ideas and concepts and expanding your knowledge base are two benefits of engaging in content analysis.

Boosting the brain's efficiency and ability to come up with new ideas through stimulating the formation of connections between disparate thoughts and concepts through data analysis and interpretation.

If you undertake the above activities, you'll always have something to write about because your mind will always be fed new frameworks from your varied experiences. Writers' block is a common topic of conversation among authors. The inability to enable your brain to make connections between different areas to generate fresh ideas is typically the result of a lack of thorough investigation and a dearth of information.

If you undertake the activities listed above, you'll always have something to write about because your mind will be constantly flooded with fresh framework from your varied experiences. Writers' block is a common topic of conversation among authors. Most of the time, this is due to a lack of information and research, which leads to opening pathways between different areas of your brain and coming up with new ideas. is an American

Stephen King is an American author who overcame writer's block to achieve phenomenal success. King's literary production fell drastically in the late 1970s as he battled alcoholism and addiction. In addition, he had just released a novel called "The Shining," which he was disappointed with.

But King persisted in his efforts, and after trying a new tactic, he was able to break through his block. He shifted his attention to the growth of his characters and wrote longer, more intricate novels in which he could delve more deeply into his themes.

This strategy paid off with the publication of "It" in 1986, a best-seller that revitalized King's career. Many of King's subsequent works have also been commercially successful. These include "The Stand," "Misery," and the "Dark Tower" series.

Thus, the initial and fundamental step to stimulate your mind is by nourishing it with a variety of information. Without sufficient knowledge stored in your mind, it's impossible to generate any new ideas.

Combining Ideas to Create Novel Concepts

the late 1970s s

Combining ideas, or "idea fusion," is a creative technique that involves combining two or more existing ideas to create something new. It can be used to generate ideas by combining two unrelated ideas, two related ideas, an existing idea with a new twist, and ideas from different cultures. By using idea fusion, you can create new and innovative concepts that have the potential to become successful business ventures or creative projects.

It's often said that if someone just had a fresh thought, it would completely alter their lives. We are constantly exposed to something brand new in the realm of technology that will completely revolutionize the way we do things.

For example, Nike's goal in the early 2000s was to design a new range of shoes that were better for the planet. The "Nike Considered" line of shoes is the result of Nike's efforts to integrate the company's established expertise for making athletic shoes with recycled materials. The use of recycled rubber, leather, and polyester in the production of these shoes demonstrates that resource efficiency was a priority. As a result of the success of the Nike Considered line, the company is now widely recognized as an innovator in eco-friendly athletic shoes.

Again, when Steve Jobs came back to Apple in 1997, he had an idea for a device that would change the face of the music industry forever. The iPod was created when Apple took the existing technology of MP3 players and merged it with a new user interface and a stylish design. As a result of the iPod's widespread popularity, Apple rose to the top of the technological sector.

Every day, it seems like a new business with a fresh take on an old problem raises millions of dollars to get off the ground.

How would you respond if you heard someone remark, "There are no new ideas," after learning about one or more innovations every day?

You will, of course, dismiss this as a foolish assertion. But suppose this assertion comes from a historical figure widely regarded as among the most inventive?

Famous American Founding Father, polymath, inventor, scientist, writer, printer, diplomat, and author Benjamin Franklin (1706–1790) once stated, "There is no new thing under the sun." According to the author of this quotation, all new ideas are really repackaged and repurposed old ones. Franklin thought that it was more effective to improve upon already-existing ideas than to try to come up with completely new ones.mo.

Ralph Waldo Emerson (1803–1882), an American essayist, lecturer, philosopher, and poet, once said "There is no such thing as a new idea. It is impossible. We simply take a lot of old ideas and put them into a sort of mental kaleidoscope." This quote emphasizes the idea that creativity and innovation often come from combining existing ideas in new and unique ways. Emerson believed that every idea had its roots in something that had come before it and that it was up to individuals to find new ways to connect those ideas and make something new.

These are the remarks with which I wholeheartedly agree.

Everything we see around us has a veneer of originality since it is founded on fresh ideas or concepts, but it is nothing more than the carefully cultivated hybridization of previously distinct concepts.

Although it is more challenging and riskier to come up with a truly original concept like sending a spaceship to another planet for tourist purposes not every idea needs to be so ambitious. That's great news for everyone, because it means that anyone who can sit quietly and watch their own mental inventory of pre-existing ideas and play around with various permutations might, in principle, come up with any new combination of ideas. T

Was Twitter some revolutionary new concept? Or of "The Adventues

When it debuted in 2006, Twitter did not introduce anything radically novel or revolutionary. Other platforms, including Jaiku and Pownce, had already experimented with the idea of microblogging, or the sharing of short updates and messages with followers.

The 140-character limit, the use of hashtags to organize material, and the focus on real-time communication and news sharing are just a few of Twitter's innovations that set it apart from its forerunners. This functionality contributed to Twitter's rise to prominence as a go-to source for real-time updates on events and celebrity happenings.

Was Instagram some revolutionary new concept?

When it was released in 2010, Instagram wasn't exactly a novel or ground-breaking concept. Before Instagram was released, there were already established options for sharing and editing photographs, such as Flickr and Instamatic for mobile devices.

Instagram, on the other hand, pioneered several ground-breaking innovations that set it apart from its contemporaries, such as its focus on mobile-first design and the use of filters to enhance and stylize photographs. Instagram's streamlined interface and ease of use also contributed to its popularity. in 2

Was Google a novel idea to become a hit in 1996 as a search engine?

When Google was first developed as a search engine in 1996, it was not a completely novel idea. At the time, there were several other search engines available, such as Yahoo, AltaVista, and Excite, that were already popular among internet users.

However, Google's founders, Larry Page, and Sergey Brin, introduced several key innovations that set it apart from its competitors. One of the most important was PageRank, a system for analysing the links between web pages and determining which pages were most relevant to a user's search query. This approach was more sophisticated than the keyword-based algorithms used by other search engines, and it helped Google provide more accurate and useful search results.

Success often goes to those who improve upon existing innovations rather than those who come up with completely new ones. Instead, those who build upon existing work have greater odds of success.

Here are some studies that compare startup success rates in the United States:

The venture capital database and analytics firm CB Insights conducted a post-mortem analysis of 101 unsuccessful businesses. The study's authors identified a lack of market need, insufficient funding, and ineffective management as the leading causes of business failure.

According to an article published in 2018 by Harvard Business Review titled "The Startup Failure Myth," the publication reviewed data from more than 1,500 technology businesses and discovered that the startup failure rate was lower than previously thought. They also discovered that funded firms had a higher failure rate than those that did not obtain venture money.

An organization for research called Statistic Brain provided startup failure rates by industry. The information sector had the highest failure rate (63.2%), followed by the banking and insurance sectors (both 58.2%), and finally the academic sector (55.5%).

The Startup Genome Project is a think tank that publishes studies on the global startup scene. Premature scaling, a lack of product-market fit, and running out of funds were identified as the primary causes of startup failure in their analysis of data from over 1 million enterprises for their 2020 report.

The failure rates of startups are shown to be very context-dependent, with factors including industry, management, funding, and product-market fit all playing significant roles. Many startups fail, but that probability can be reduced through thoughtful market research, prudent resource management, and a relentless emphasis on satisfying customers' wants and requirements. Therefore, to be creative thinker, you don't have to be first. You just must be different and better. Therefore, originality in thought is more important than being first. You only need to be superior and unique.

How does combining different ideas work?

The process of combining two or more separate ideas into one novel thought involves combining concepts from multiple areas of study and identifying areas of agreement. It involves single out the many notions that will make up the whole, seeking out connections between them, reframing the ideas, and merging the two concepts into a single, ground-breaking idea. This can lead to breakthroughs in business, resolution of difficult problems, and enhancement of people's quality of life.

Let's look at a few instances where the combination of different concepts led to the development of revolutionary new ideas.

The creation of the United States represents one of the earliest examples of a synthesis of ideas in the Americas. Some of the sources that influenced the founding fathers were the ideas of Enlightenment philosophers, the political systems of ancient Greece and Rome, and the founders' own colonial experiences.

Democracy, individual freedom, and representative government by fusing these seemingly disparate notions, a new political system was born. The United States was founded on this synthesis of ideas, which has had far-reaching effects on the evolution of political and social systems across the globe.

Let's take another real-life example.

American entrepreneur and inventor Sylvan Nathan Goldman was born in Ardmore, Oklahoma, on November 15, 1898. The first shopping cart was invented by him in 1936 and completely changed the retail industry. Goldman, who ran a chain of supermarkets in Oklahoma, noticed that his customers often bought only as much as they could carry in their arms. To solve this problem, he invented the shopping cart so that buyers could stack multiple items into a single transaction. The shopping cart was an instant hit, and within a few years, they were ubiquitous in supermarkets throughout the United States. Throughout his life, Goldman continued to invent new things and secure patents for them, which led to his induction into the National Inventors Hall of Fame in 2005.

In another example, Kurt Vonnegut an American writer who successfully combined disparate elements. Science fiction, satire, and social commentary all found their way into Vonnegut's writings. His best-known work, "Slaughterhouse Five," deals with such diverse topics as time travel, combat, and anti-war sentiment. His time as a prisoner of war in WWII and his career in public relations for General Electric both served as sources of motivation for him. Vonnegut's novel-writing style was ground breaking since it included elements from numerous literary traditions.

The Harvard Business Review published an important study on the value of idea fusion in 2013. According to the research, aggressively encouraging idea fusion and the exchange of ideas between departments and employees can foster a culture of innovation and success. The study also discovered that teams that are demographically and skill-set-diverse are more likely to engage in idea fusion and produce more novel ideas. According to the findings, merging ideas can produce game-changing breakthroughs that give businesses an edge in today's cutthroat marketplace. Already

I hope the above illustrations were helpful in stimulating your own creative thinking.

Let's observe how the process of mental amalgamation works.

The ability to generate new ideas relies more on synthesis than analysis. The key is to make connections where none previously existed, to look for the big picture rather than the small details, and to come up with novel solutions by pairing items that have never been put together before. Est

As was mentioned before, the left hemisphere is more analytical, and the right hemisphere is responsible for synthesis of ideas.ablished

Let's talk about Numerous strategies that exist for rapidly producing large numbers of ideas.

Mind Mapping:

The purpose of mind mapping is to facilitate the visual organization of thoughts and concepts. It entails drawing a diagram that links ideas, concepts, and conceptions through a central node that stands for the main topic or idea. Subtopics radiate out from the initial node and are linked to the rest of the diagram by lines or branches. Information can be organized hierarchically by breaking it down into smaller, more manageable chunks, such as these subtopics.

By aiding in ideation, organization, and clarity, as well as memory and recall, mind mapping serves a useful purpose. Brainstorming, problem-solving, project planning, and even taking notes can all benefit from the use of mind maps.

You can create a mind map by hand, or you can use dedicated software. A mind map can be created either independently or in a collaborative setting, making it useful in a variety of contexts. He

Brainstorming:

Brainstorming is a time-efficient method of coming up with creative solutions to problems. In a group situation, people are free to voice whatever random thoughts occur to them without being judged on their accuracy or potential usefulness.

Brainstorming is a technique used to come up with several different approaches to a problem or to achieve a goal. Participants are expected to collaborate with one another to generate novel ideas and approaches.

Traditional brainstorming and online brainstorming are the two most common approaches to coming up with new ideas. Conventional brainstorming sessions often involve a group of people sitting in a room and trading verbal suggestions. Participants in an electronic brainstorming session all contribute ideas to a common document or online forum.

In many industries, including business, education, and others, brainstorming has proven to be a useful tool for coming up with fresh and original concepts. It's crucial to remember, though, that not every good idea comes from a brainstorming session. After a brainstorming session, it is up to the group or individual to assess and improve upon the ideas that were developed.

SCAMPER:

SCAMPER is a creative thinking technique used to generate ideas and solutions to problems. It is an acronym for substitute, combine, adapt, modify, put to another use, eliminate, and reverse. The technique was first introduced by Alex Osborn, a well-known advertising executive and co-founder of the Creative Education Foundation.

Each letter of the acronym represents a different way to approach a problem and generate ideas. For example:

Substitute: Think about substituting one element of the problem with something else.

Combine: Think about combining different elements or ideas to create something new.

Adapt: Think about how the problem or solution could be adapted or changed to fit a different context.

Modify: Think about modifying or changing one or more elements of the problem or solution.

Put it to another use: Think about how the problem or solution could be used in a different context or for a different purpose.

Eliminate: Think about what elements of the problem or solution could be eliminated or removed.

Reverse: Think about reversing the order or direction of the problem or solution.

The goal of SCAMPER is to stimulate creative thinking and generate a wide range of ideas and solutions. It can be used individually or in a group setting and is often used in brainstorming sessions or as part of a larger creative problem-solving process.

Reverse Thinking:

Reverse thinking, often called reverse brainstorming or reverse ideation, is a method of addressing problems by inverting the usual way of thinking. Instead of asking, "What can we do to solve this problem?" or "How can we achieve this goal?" reverse thinkers ask, "What could we do to make this problem worse?" or "What actions could we take to prevent us from achieving our goal?" Reverse thinking is analysing the inverse of a problem or solution to better understand it and come up with novel approaches to resolving it. It can also be useful for questioning preconceived notions and stimulating fresh approaches to an issue.

Random word association:

Another way to generate fresh and original ideas is using the "random word association" technique. Choosing a word at random and then coming up with ideas or associations based on that word is what this method is all about. This can be done singly or in a group, with participants taking turns offering suggestions based on the chosen word.

If the chosen word is "tree," for instance, the group might offer up synonyms such as "shade," "oxygen," "lumber," "nature," "leaves," "branches," "bird habitat," and so on. The objective is to come up with as many ideas as possible, regardless of how unlikely or irrelevant they may seem at first. By challenging people to go outside their comfort zones and consider ideas in new ways, this method can be useful for fostering innovation and fresh perspectives. e way to ate

Forced Connections:

If you're stuck for an idea or need a solution to an issue, try using the "forced connections" strategy, which entails finding two unconnected things and making a connection between them. To develop fresh and original ideas, this method relies on fusing seemingly disparate thoughts together.

To make use of forced connections, pick out two things that have nothing in common at first. To come up with fresh concepts, you next look for links between them. If you were brainstorming for a new product, you might decide to merge the ideas of a bicycle with a computer to come up with the concept of a "smart bike" that employs GPS and other sensors to keep track of your rides and give you immediate feedback on how you're doing.

Because it compels you to investigate ideas you might not have otherwise considered, forced connections can be an effective strategy for generating new concepts. By fusing seemingly unconnected ideas, you can generate ground-breaking approaches to old challenges, setting you apart from the competition and fuelling your company's success. Oos

Six Thinking Hats: Maltese physician, psychologist, and consultant Edward de Bono created the Six Thinking Hats framework. Its goal is to facilitate better thought processes by exposing participants to new ways of thinking.

The six "hats" reflect several ways of thinking:

The white hat stands for an unbiased approach that is data driven. It takes a cold, analytical look at the world, removing all emotional considerations.

The red hat stands for sentimental considerations and intuitive insights. It's a way for people to say what's really on their minds and hearts.

Black hat stands for critical thought, which is centered on foreseeing and eliminating roadblocks. It takes a cautious and negative view of the world.

Optimistic and solution-oriented, the yellow hat is associated with this mindset. It takes a bright and optimistic view of the world. in a

In the end, the specifics of the project or challenge at hand will determine the ideal approach or technique for rapidly producing many ideas. To maximize the possibility of producing original and significant solutions, it is important to maintain an open mind and actively seek out a variety of ideas and perspectives. egies exist for

Let's discuss about two idea generation techniques in detail with examples. Gr

Use Brainstorming Method to Quickly Generate Many Ideas

Brainstorming is a time-efficient method of coming up with creative solutions to problems.

Alex Osborn, an advertising executive, created the brainstorming approach in the late 1930s and popularized it in his 1953 book "Applied Imagination." Osborn believed in the ability of collaborative creativity to develop ideas; therefore, he co-founded the advertising agency BBDO (Batten, Barton, Durstine, & Osborn). To facilitate creative problem-solving and teamwork, he formally established the brainstorming process. Since then, many different industries have adopted the practice of brainstorming to generate ideas and solve problems more easily.

Here is a step-by-step guide on how to use the brainstorming method:

Get set and establish your goal: First, you need to pinpoint the issue or goal for which you require solutions. Put it down on paper in as much detail as possible. For instance, "conceive of some novel advertising strategies."

Collect a wide range of people: Gather a team that has a wide range of experiences, opinions, and knowledge in the area. Diverse viewpoints and experiences should be actively sought.

Make the atmosphere comfortable: Create a setting that allows you to kick back and think beyond the obvious. Find somewhere private where people won't be interrupted while they're talking.

Lay forth the regulations: Lay out some guidelines for how this session of brainstorming will operate. Make it clear that there will be no rejection or evaluation of ideas during this brainstorming session. Inspire people to share their thoughts and build upon the work of others.

Warm Up: Get everyone in an open and receptive frame of mind by beginning with a creative warm-up exercise. This can take the form of a brief task or a related icebreaker question.

Generate Ideas: Encourage participants to come up with as many ideas as they can in each amount of time (say, 15 to 20 minutes). Tell them to stop limiting their ideas and stifling their creativity. If you need to, use outside prompts or stimuli to get your brain working.

Encourage Free Flow of Ideas: Help people feel comfortable sharing their thoughts and remind them that quantity is more important than quality at this point. Ignore analysing or debating ideas until the idea creation phase is complete, and instead encourage them to build upon one another's ideas.

Record all ideas: Compile your thoughts. Make sure everyone can see the ideas being discussed by writing them down on a whiteboard, flip chart, or digital platform. Don't filter or judge your ideas; just write them down. This graphic aid keeps people interested and encourages new ideas.

Group and Cluster ideas: After the brainstorming stage is complete, it's time to group and cluster the ideas for a group discussion. Examine the ideas to see if there are any connections or themes. Create clusters of related concepts.

Discuss and refine: Talk about and improve: Create a safe space for people to share their thoughts, ask questions, and build on the ideas of others. Get people to elaborate on their thoughts, make suggestions for improvement, and mix and match their ideas to come up with fresh perspectives.

Evaluate and Prioritize: Following the meeting, evaluate the suggestions in terms of their feasibility, impact, and how well they connect with the overall goal. Give more time and resources to the most promising and applicable ideas.

Follow up actions: Based on the concepts you've chosen, decide what to do next. Define roles, establish timelines, and create a strategy for moving forward with research or execution.

Let's take example of Apple. The creation of the Apple iPod is a practical application of the brainstorming process. Apple's iPod was developed in response to consumer demand for a portable digital music player with an intuitive interface. Apple's staff, including Steve Jobs, held a few brainstorming sessions to discuss the problem and come up with ideas for how to approach it.

Members of the team were encouraged to speak their minds and provide ideas during the brainstorming sessions. Design, functionality, user interface, and storage capacity were only a few of the topics they covered with regards to the digital music player.

The group discussed many ideas and options through brainstorming. They used the variety of their experiences and knowledge to come up with fresh concepts. Ideas such as a user-friendly touchscreen interface, straightforward menus, and a small footprint emerged from these discussions.

The team's focus on the user experience was a major turning point in the brainstorming session. They pictured a gadget with room for hundreds of songs, easy controls like a scroll wheel, and a sleek, attractive form factor. They were able to hone these concepts and ideas through a series of brainstorming sessions.

The current iteration of the iPod was developed through a series of brainstorming meetings that encouraged open discussion and teamwork. The finished product was stylish, user-friendly, and capable of holding a large music collection.

The success of the iPod is evidence that group discussion can stimulate creative thinking. Apple's ability to transform the digital music industry and produce a product that fundamentally changed the way people listen to music is a direct result of the company's openness to multiple perspectives and the free flow of ideas.

To see how effective collaborative idea generation can be and how it may have a transformative effect on businesses, consider the role that brainstorming played in the creation of the iPod.

Use SCAMPER Method to Quickly Generate Many Ideas

The SCAMPER technique provides a set of questions meant to stimulate creative thinking. It offers a method that provides students with a framework for thinking creatively.

Alex Faickney Osborn, an advertising executive and author, first proposed the SCAMPER approach in 1953; in 1971, Bob Eberle published SCAMPER: Games for Imagination Development, which expanded upon Osborn's work.

With this seven-letter acronym in mind, break down your problem or project into manageable chunks, and then brainstorm solutions by asking yourself the following questions at each level:

S = **Substitute** something

C= **Combine** it with something else.

A = **Adapt** something to it

M = **Modify** or magnify it

P = **Put it** to some different use.

E = **Eliminate** something

R = **Reverse** engineer it.

Use of the SCAMPER Method

First, you'll need to break the problem down into manageable chunks.

Second, integrate the SCAMPER method's seven components into your project's questioning and ideation processes at each level.

Let's try it out with a made-up scenario to illustrate how this method could be used in the real world.

Consider the difficulty of opening a successful book franchise.

Step one is to dissect the problem into manageable chunks. These are some of the possible next steps for this company.

1. Finding a popular book franchise or brand in your

neighbourhood where people congregate for meetings, work, or just to enjoy a book is step number one. You should make sure there is a decent chance of foot traffic, and that the franchisor is willing to give you a fair cut of the profits.

2. Sign the franchise agreement after successful negotiations with the franchisor.

3. Identifying an ideal commercial site and negotiating a favourable leasing agreement.

4. Promote your book shop and encourage people to stop by.b

d

Let's take one of your project's phases and use the SCAMPER technique to brainstorm some additional ideas. Consider these questions as you plan to advertise your soon-to-open book store:

- **Where can I find an alternative to my current methods of promotion and customer invitation?**

I was wondering whether there was a cheaper alternative to the current method of distributing pamphlets in newspapers and other offline periodicals, such as on Facebook, Instagram, or any of the other popular social media sites.

- **Is there anything else you can do to supplement your current advertising strategy?**

You might encourage people to tell their friends about your book store by offering discounts to both returning customers and newcomers in the form of referral coupons that they could distribute online.

- **What other parts of the advertising strategies of already successful businesses can I steal?**

Should you consider providing first-time customers with a discount coupon for their following two visits?

- **How can I improve or expand my marketing strategy?**

To increase the effectiveness of your campaign, you may want to consider inviting a local celebrity or influencer to your book store (which could be costly) and having them share the event with their social media followers.

- **Where else can I apply my marketing skills?**

By giving monthly discounts, you can use your marketing efforts to turn first-time customers into repeat buyers and secure a steady stream of revenue.

- **What barriers can you remove from your current method of customer invitation?**

Perhaps you don't need to spend so much on traditional advertising methods if you focus on creating viral content instead.

Is there anything you might do backwards or differently to make your business more welcoming to new customers? You might encourage people to tell heir friends bout your café by offering discounts to and newcomers in the

Consider the possibility that, as an alternative to your own advertising, your customers could spread the news about your business for free. For instance, the book store may provide a 15% discount to everyone who posts a photo of themselves enjoying their time there on Instagram or Facebook and tags the store's social media profile. This is sure to pique the interest of today's youth, whether they are in high school or college. In this approach, clients will spread the word about your business by referring their friends and family. With more people talking about your page, the social media platform's algorithm will start to favor you, which means you'll get greater organic reach for less money.

The SCAMPER method of generating multiple ideas by using a prescribed series of questions to generate a wide range of responses has just been demonstrated to you.

To illustrate how this scamper process began creating all those fantastic ideas by activating minor prompts, I'll use the example of building a book store, even though I have no current intentions to do so.

In addition, in our example, we only applied this method to the first step of your business idea; if you apply it to other stages, you'll find yourself inundated with new and improved concepts.

Your mind has an infinite capacity that needs to be tapped by asking the right set of questions, and that's exactly what the SCAMPER method does. Subtle triggers provided by SCAMPER prompt your mind to generate a wide range of potential solutions.

Tips for putting scammers into practice in your daily life.

Consider one of the truly important endeavours you hope to complete with the help of your own unique brand of creative problem-solving. After you've settled on a plan, break it down into as many manageable chunks as you can think of so that each one may be evaluated independently.

Now, apply the SCAMPER questions to a single phase of your project, writing down answers and other thoughts as they come to you.

Apply SCAMPER to each strategy and continue to jot down any ideas that come to mind as you go.

Examine the results of your brainstorming as soon as possible. I have no doubt that you will generate far more ideas than you would through regular mental processing alone. You can see the difference for yourself if you try it out.

Let's try something different now to get our creative ideas flowing.

The Advantages of Creative Multitasking

Contrary to common perception, research on the topic of multitasking and productivity has found that it might have a negative effect on productivity. Here are some major conclusions drawn from studies:

Efficiency Loss Because switching between jobs requires time and mental energy, it reduces productivity. Researchers at Stanford University showed that, compared to those who focused on a single task at a time, multitaskers were slower and made more mistakes.

Multitasking reduces efficiency since it requires more mental effort to keep track of everything you're doing at once. The capacity to ignore distractions and stay focused both suffered in those who multitasked, according to a study published in the Journal of Experimental Psychology: Human Perception and Performance.

Reduced Efficiency Multitasking has been linked to a drop in efficiency at work. It takes an average of 23 minutes and 15 seconds to go back into the zone after being interrupted, according to research out of the University of California, Irvine. Constantly shifting focus from one activity to another might impede productivity.

Some people may believe they are effective multitaskers, but studies have shown that concentrating on a single activity at a time and avoiding interruptions results in greater efficiency and higher output overall. Productivity and efficiency at work can be improved by switching to single-tasking and employing techniques like time management, prioritizing, and limiting distractions.

However, there is a form of multitasking that is advised for allowing for the emergence of creative thought. Let me elaborate by pointing to some of history's brightest lights who have mastered this brand of multitasking. What other parts of the advertising strategies of already successful

Albert Einstein's breakthrough physics work has received the most attention, he really worked on and finished several other projects during his lifetime. Key elements of Einstein's methodology that allowed him to successfully handle several projects include the following:

Einstein was very efficient with his time and knew how to set priorities. So that he wouldn't fall behind on any of his projects, he scheduled out certain chunks of time to work on each.

Einstein had a strong capacity for prioritizing. He would prioritize the most crucial initiatives, giving his all to those that needed his attention right away or held the key to major advances.

Einstein understood the importance of teamwork, so he frequently collaborated with other researchers, scientists, and students. He was able to accomplish more by focusing on fewer things, thanks to his strategy of outsourcing certain tasks and working with others.

Although Einstein worked on many different projects, many of them were related to or built upon each other, creating a synergistic effect. By applying what he learned in one attempt to another, he was able to generate momentum in all his pursuits.

When working on a project, Einstein would give his complete attention to it. He used intense concentration and careful thought to peel back the layers of the issue at hand and arrive at some novel insights.

Einstein made strategic use of his downtime because he understood its worth. He frequently allowed his thoughts to wander during downtime, which served as a time for the unconscious processing and incubation of ideas. This mental revitalization was critical to his success in juggling several tasks.

Einstein was willing to take in new information and adjust his methods accordingly. He would refine and deepen his understanding by applying what he had learned to new initiatives.

While Einstein did work on numerous tasks, he did not multitask at the same time. Instead, he gave his undivided attention to each individual task at hand. By planning and setting realistic goals, he was able to make substantial contributions to a wide range of scientific fields. Businesses can I steal?

Let's take another example.

Elon Musk a well-known businessman and visionary who has contributed to the development of several innovative firms. He is known for his practice of delegating authority and assembling capable teams to carry out day-to-day tasks. He is also known for his hard work ethic and disciplined routine, and his knowledge and expertise span several fields. He has spoken openly about the difficulties and compromises that come with multitasking, but his status as a significant figure associated with multitasking has been cemented by his ability to oversee and push development across numerous major undertakings.

What exactly is going on?

Don't misunderstand me. No one was performing multiple, dissimilar jobs simultaneously. They didn't think multitasking like that was possible. Instead, they were multitasking, although slowly.

The best artists in their field jump from one genre to another, but why do they do this? Or, to rephrase the question, how can sluggish multitasking increase productivity?

These are the justifications:

If they get stuck on one project, they can go on to another while still making progress overall.

In 1915, for instance, Einstein's efforts in the field of general relativity had worn him down, so he switched gears. He was able to work out a solution to his theory of relativity by shifting his focus to something else for a while.

After some time away from the primary task, he returned to it with renewed energy and a fresh perspective.

- Humans have a desire for novelty, which can be satisfied by switching between different undertakings, which provides mental variety and stimulation. It's a great way to break up the monotony, boost your brainpower, and foster some very original brainstorming. By working on a wide variety of tasks, people can improve their knowledge and abilities without tiring their minds out. Motivation is boosted and boredom is avoided when workers are often exposed to new challenges by switching between projects.

- This method of slow multitasking might be thought of as mental cross-training. Think of it like training for a half marathon. You don't have to go for a run every single day. On non-running days, you engage in cross-training to give your body essential flexibility and to rest your leg muscles. Changing your focus from one task to another and back again is like cross-training for your brain; you'll feel revitalized and ready to tackle the first task again.

- Now, learning to master one skill improves your ability to master others.

That's why, if we want to improve significantly, it's necessary to take frequent breaks from the main project.

A study showed that highly regarded researchers changed their focus an average of 43% of the time within their first 100 papers.

Multitasking has made Elon Musk, an American business magnate, famous. Elon Musk is an entrepreneur, inventor, and engineer who has worked on multiple projects at once. He established SpaceX as CEO and chief designer, Tesla, Inc. as CEO and chief product architect, Neuralink as CEO, and The Boring Company as founder. In addition to SpaceX and Tesla, Musk is also working on SolarCity and OpenAI. His multitasking skills have garnered him praise for his ability to oversee and steer several businesses at once while driving them all toward lofty objectives. This is a good example of slow multi-tasking and working on different projects all together.

Debbie Allen an American choreographer known for multitasking. Debbie Allen is a renowned dancer, choreographer, actress, and director. She has been involved in numerous projects simultaneously, showcasing her multitasking abilities. Allen has choreographed for various TV shows, films, and stage productions, including the television series "Fame," for which she won several Emmy Awards. In addition to her choreography work, she has also acted in films and television shows, directed episodes of popular TV series, and served as a producer. Allen's diverse talents and ability to juggle multiple roles and responsibilities exemplify her multitasking skills in the entertainment industry.onsider providing free Wi-Fi for the first two hours, as some cafés do, or

Through effective time management, organizational skills, and a deep passion for her craft, Debbie Allen has been able to excel in multiple roles simultaneously. Her ability to switch between choreography, acting, directing, and producing demonstrates her slow multitasking prowess in the entertainment industry. Two visits?

You can see that she never loses a creative notion through slow multitasking, and she also doesn't have to limit her creative thinking to the one thing she's working on at the moment.

It's impossible to predict which of your life's newfound passions will trigger the creative discoveries that will prove to be priceless.

When and how should you use this method? Or expa

Prioritize tasks: Tasks should be prioritized based on importance and urgency rather than attempted simultaneously. Just do what you need to do, and then move on to the next thing. This way, you may offer each task your undivided focus and energy, increasing the likelihood of a successful outcome.

Practice mindfulness: Maintain concentration by paying close attention to the here and now. Don't let anything pull your focus away from the task at hand. This aids in keeping your mind from wandering, enhancing the quality of your work, and decreasing the frequency with which you transition between tasks.

Time blocking: Block off chunks of time on your calendar and use them for specific endeavours. By setting out this specific time, you can focus on a single project until it's completed. You can do more and feel less overwhelmed if you make a plan that sets aside time for each activity.

Single-tasking: Adopt the practice of "single-tasking," in which you give your full attention to a single activity until it is finished. Turn off notifications or schedule times when you can check your inbox and messages to keep disruptions to a minimum.

Break tasks into smaller steps: Tasks that are too vast or too complicated should be broken down into smaller, more manageable chunks. Taking things one step at a time will help you get things done without getting overwhelmed. Maintaining such focus and clarity throughout the procedure is facilitated by this method.

Take care of yourself: If you want to keep your mind sharp and your body healthy, you need to practice self-care. Make breaks, rest, and relaxation top priorities to restore your energy. Stress can be reduced, and concentration improved by taking time out for physical activity, meditation, or a favourite pastime.

Schedule some time to reflect alone: It's preferable to schedule some alone time for a creative walk and journaling. During a holiday, you should take some time to unwind alone, preferably for at least an hour.d

Schedule walking session: Keep on walking and reflect on the things you've started but never finished since you didn't want to give them your all at the time. Perhaps you could have made a difference if you had written a book, composed a song, written a poem, or run for office in your condominium association. You either didn't begin because you knew it would detract from your primary task or you abandoned it quickly after getting started. After giving it some thought, jot down quick bullet points of whatever ideas come to mind on your phone or notepad. You may just say what's on your mind and jot notes on your phone's recorder. Don't ignore any of these possibilities; you may find yourself with new tasks soon. Walk for an hour. Walking for an hour is the kind of activity that will tire you out physically and emotionally.

Get ready for your journaling session by unwinding at home after your walk. Get a notebook and put your name inside a circle drawn in the middle of a blank page. Now you need to make a mental map of your projects, with branches radiating out from the center and space for sub-branches to grow from there. Some possible examples of branch types are:

- Value you give to society.
- Your physical well-being.
- Your long-held dreams of making a meaningful contribution to the world.
- Your children's development-related projects

Now that you have your list of projects, you may begin highlighting them according to their category by using different coloured markers or pens, or you can use the same pen to assign each project a unique identification number, such as A1, A2, A3, etc. If you wanted to organize your tasks by deadline, you might use categories like

- What can be initiated from today onward?
- A few weeks from now.
- in the next six months.
- In the next year.
- Perhaps later.

You'll gain enough insight from this to know which side projects would be a good addition to your primary ones.

It's possible that you'll sign up for a language study course tomorrow or perhaps begin taking local music or dancing lessons.

Test out slow multitasking and see how it improves your main activity, allowing you to take in more information and complete more tasks. inside a circle drawn in the middle of a blank page. Now you need to make a

Make Yourself an Idea Generator: Establish a Daily Idea Limit

Thomas Edison is a famous American inventor who gained fame for his prolific idea generation. Edison was a successful businessman and innovator who amassed over a thousand patents for his numerous creations. His team's goal was to come up with a small idea every 10 days and a significant invention every six months.branch

Brian Tracy is an internationally recognized motivational speaker and best-selling author of books on self-improvement and business success. In his book "Maximum Achievement," Brian Tracy recommends keeping a daily idea journal in which you record 10 new concepts or thoughts.

Scott Adams, the man behind the wildly successful "Dilbert" comic strip, has also written several books about management and self-improvement. Adams, in his book "How to Fail at Almost Everything and Still Win Big," advocates for the practice of regular idea generation to boost one's chances of success and maintain flexibility in the face of a volatile and unpredictable environment.

Building up a creative mind is like working up your body. Strength training with increasing weight and stretching are the cornerstones of any muscle-building program. The same holds true for your thoughts and concepts. Challenge your creativity by setting a daily goal of coming up with a certain number of new ideas.

It takes time, energy, and a flexible mind to develop into a perpetual source of new ideas. The ability to generate a steady stream of ideas is useful in various contexts, including business, issue solving, and personal development.

You might be wondering what sort of concepts we're discussing.

In order to attract fresh ideas, you must first have a clear problem and turn it into a challenge, as I mentioned earlier. Therefore, the concepts should be pertinent to your fundamental issues.

When making a creative decision, more options usually mean better ones.

The more ideas generated, the better they will be. Rather than hoping inspiration will strike, developing a routine in which you produce a certain number of ideas every day will train your brain to be more productive.

The first step is to come up with five ideas related to your difficulties every day for a week. The process will be challenging at first, but as you begin writing, the dots will begin to connect, and greater ideas will emerge.

Then, evaluate the ideas you've developed this week and pick the best ones to incorporate into your major tasks.

There is a good chance that you will find at least one good idea that can be put into immediate use on your most pressing projects.

Here are some things few of them we have already discussed that you can do to improve your ability to think of new ideas:

Encourage a mind that is curious: Curiosity is the fuel that keeps the creative juices flowing. Develop your natural inquisitiveness, question things, and learn about the world around you. Get out there and talk to people from all walks of life, as well as read books, articles, and blogs. The more information and experiences you have, the better able you are to draw conclusions and come up with new ideas.

Make it a point to generate ideas: Schedule dedicated time and establish objectives for brainstorming. Set aside time each day or week to focus entirely on creative thinking and idea generation. Maintaining a consistent routine is like exercising your imagination.

Practice brainstorming techniques: You can improve your ability to develop new ideas by engaging in a variety of brainstorming exercises. Mind mapping, free writing, and the SCAMPER method

(Substitute, Combine, Adapt, Modify, Put to Another Use, Eliminate, Reverse) are all well-liked approaches. Try out various approaches until you find the one that works best for you.

Embrace divergent thinking: Embrace the practice of diverse thinking, which entails considering many different perspectives and options. Try not to settle for just one answer or strategy. Instead, force yourself to come up with as many ideas as you can, even if some of them are completely out there. Quality usually follows quantity because one thought can motivate another.

Diversify your sources for ideas: Put yourself in situations where you're subjected to a wide variety of inputs. Interact with people from diverse fields and cultures. Participate in meetings, seminars, and workshops. Investigate the world through various mediums. If you have a wide range of places to go for ideas, you'll come up with a wide range of concepts.

Develop idea-capturing habits: Habitually recording your ideas is important because inspiration might strike at any time. Keep a notebook on hand or utilize a note-taking program on your mobile device so that you may write down ideas as soon as they strike. Make a plan to frequently analyse your progress and refine your strategy. Even if at first glance an idea seems absurd, it could prove useful in the long run or when combined with other ideas.

Collaborate and discuss ideas: Participate in group brainstorming sessions and openly share your own ideas with others to speed up the creative process. Find a community of creative thinkers, a mastermind group, or a brainstorming session to join. In group settings, people's thoughts and opinions tend to meld and grow.

Embrace failure and iteration: Accept that not all your initial ideas will pan out and be open Embrace failure and iteration: to adjusting as necessary. Take setbacks in stride and use them as learning opportunities. Take everything you've learned and used to enhance your ideas over time. Every setback is a stepping stone to future successes.

Take Action: Just thinking about something isn't enough; you need to do something about it. Pick the best ideas from your pile and get to work on making them a reality. Put your theories to the test in the real world and tweak them there. This method will aid in your education, adaptation, and future idea production.

Keep in mind that developing your ability to generate ideas quickly takes time and effort. You may develop your creative potential and become a prolific source of unique ideas by regularly participating in idea generation exercises, cultivating your curiosity, and exposing yourself to a wide range of experiences.es to g

martphone

Chapter 5 Key Takeaways med

Embrace boredom to foster idea generation. When you're bored, you're not driven by your constant desires and distractions. You will experience boredom if you do nothing. The DMN, or imagining network, of your brain is triggered when you allow yourself to become bored.dusk

Nourish your mind extensively before you try to generate completely new ideas. "The function of education is to teach one to think intensively and critically. Intelligence plus character—that is the goal of true education." Martin Luther King Jr. Reading widely, particularly biographies and works on topics outside of one's own expertise, might help cultivate an environment in which new ideas can flourish.

Combining Ideas to Create Novel Concepts. There is a lack of original thought, and most innovations merely improve upon or combine past developments. Now that you've stuffed your brain with ideas, it's time to start putting them to use. Using a technique like mind mapping to get your scattered thoughts down on paper can help you better combine them.

Use Brainstorming Method to Quickly Generate Many Ideas. It fosters an atmosphere where people feel comfortable expressing their ideas without worrying about being criticised or dismissed. That independence allows for the discovery of novel approaches that would not have been possible with more conventional ways of thinking.

Use the SCAMPER method. Using this strategy, you'll have access to seven distinct ways of inquiring into your own character. To come up with new ideas, you can use the letters in the acronym SCAMPER to come up with questions to ask.

The Advantages of Creative Multitasking. Instead of constantly switching between different jobs, you should immerse yourself in multiple projects at once. This allows you to take a step back from the task at hand, clearing your head so that you can come up with more refined solutions. Working on many tasks together also allows you to accomplish more.

Establish a daily idea limit. You should set a goal to come up with at least five new ideas for your tasks or problems every day. Having good ideas requires daily exercise. The higher the quantity of ideas from which to choose, the higher the quality of the ideas you'll ultimately choose.

around, it's almost time for it to drain. The same thing happens to your energy if you constantly shift it between different activities.

ng?

Chapter 6: Effective Methods for Creative Problem Solving

****

"The significant problems we face cannot be solved at the same level of thinking we were at when we created them."
- Albert Einstein

You learned a lot of creative thinking techniques in the last chapters. I hope you will find these suggestions helpful and put them into practise. Let's keep looking at some additional ways to stimulate your imagination.

Verify all Defaults and Assumptions

Elon Musk is a real-life example of how questioning established norms and challenging conventional knowledge can lead to success. He has challenged assumptions and pushed limits in several different businesses, causing significant disruption. He also defied conventional wisdom about space travel, making it affordable for the masses and expanding humanity's reach into other solar systems. Elon Musk challenged the status quo and thought creatively to create reusable rockets and SolarCity to make solar power more affordable for homes. This strategy enabled him to launch innovative businesses and make important contributions to the development of electric vehicles, space travel, and renewable energy.

Steve Jobs, the co-founder of Apple Inc., was admired for his willingness to question established norms and pursue innovation at any costs. He challenged conventional wisdom throughout his career, leading to the creation of ground-breaking products and Apple's phenomenal growth. He was responsible for releasing the Apple II in the 1970s, the Macintosh in the 1980s, and the iPod in the early 2000s. His method of challenging assumptions and exploring creative ideas has left an indelible mark on the IT sector and the way we use technology every day.

Take another example. The American craft beer industry is an example of a successful industry where every default or assumption is questioned. In the 1980s and 1990s, craft brewers began to question traditional brewing techniques and locally sourced ingredients, emphasising flavour, originality, and quality. This has led to a thriving subculture of beer lovers who value craft beer.

When it comes to having doubts about assumptions, there are a few usual ones:

Validity Doubt: This type of doubt asks if an idea is correct, true, or true enough.

Relevance doubt: Relevance doubt is when you question whether an assumption is relevant or applicable to a certain scenario or context.

Assumption challenging: Assumption challenging is the process of constantly questioning and looking into the assumptions that are being made.

Counterfactual doubt: Counterfactual doubt is when you think about other possible outcomes or situations that counter or question the assumption.

Contextual Doubt: When there is contextual doubt, the situation in which the assumption is made is called into question.

Cultural or social doubt: cultural or social doubt is when you question ideas that are based on cultural or social norms, biases, or beliefs.

The above questions encourage introspection and the testing of assumptions. By challenging preconceived notions, we open ourselves up to alternative perspectives and methods of problem-solving.

Multiple academic investigations have questioned long-held beliefs; for example, the Stanford Prison Experiment and Jennifer L. Eberhardt's study of unconscious prejudice in law enforcement Scientists can learn more and do more by constantly questioning and challenging their own assumptions as part of their research and critical thinking.

Therefore, if you want to be more creative and come up with new ideas, you should:

- Stop thinking that default choices are the only way to go. If someone suggests a product or service, for example, if he or she is using it, you don't have to accept their usual choice right away. Instead, you should ask questions and investigate the other choices as well.
- You need to make it a habit to question what people tell you. People usually think that every worker needs to be there for

8 hours. But have you ever wondered why each worker had to work the same number of hours? You could ask, "What if someone finishes their work in 4 hours? Why shouldn't they be able to use that time to meet someone outside of the office, go to an event or programme, or meet new people who can bring more business to the organisation?"

The first step to making something new is to question what people usually do. If you are happy with how things are, you won't think of ways to make them better. So, you should start to question the ideas more often to give your mind a challenge to do better. it comes to having

Questions. Questions. Questions = Ideas. Ideas and Thoughts

When they come across a problem or issue, great innovators always ask questions, and they ask many kinds of questions.

Questions and ideas go together because they are the first step in coming up with new ones. They encourage people to be curious, to question what they think they know, to think in different ways, to solve problems, to talk to each other, and to work together. Questions make people want to find out more, test their ideas, think in different ways, solve problems, talk to each other, and work together.

"The quality of your life is in direct proportion to the quality of the questions you ask yourself." - Tony Robbins

"If I had an hour to solve a problem and my life depended on the solution, I would spend the first 55 minutes determining the proper question to ask, for once I know the proper question, I could solve the problem in less than five minutes." - Albert Einstein

Isaac Newton asked, "Why does an apple fall from a tree?" and, "Why does the moon not fall into the Earth?"

Eric Schmidt, Executive Chairman of Google's parent company, Alphabet, once said, "We run this company on questions, not answers."

American author and systems thinker Peter Senge talks about "The Focusing Question" in his book "The Fifth Discipline: The Art and Practise of the Learning Organisation." The book looks at the idea of making organisations that learn and keep getting better. Senge talks about how important it is to ask thoughtful and deep questions that help people and organisations focus on their goals and make real change. umptions, there are a few usual ones:

Gary Keller is another well-known American author who writes about "The Focusing Question." He wrote the book "The ONE Thing: The Surprisingly Simple Truth Behind Extraordinary Results" with Jay

Papasan. Keller talks about the "focusing question" in his book. The idea is to find the most important job or goal that will make everything else easier or unnecessary and put it at the top of your list. The question that helps you focus is, "What's the one thing I can do that will make everything else easier or unnecessary if I do it?" Keller looks at how this question can help people be successful and productive in different parts of life and work.

Validity Doubt: This type of doubt asks if an idea is correct, true, or true enough. It ans You can come up with new ideas every day by asking yourself a variety of questions that get you to think creatively and try new things. Here are some examples:

What new options can I investigate today?

How can I look at this problem from an entirely new angle?

What can I learn from a mistake or loss I've made recently?

What would happen if I put together two thoughts or concepts that don't go together?

How can I speed up or make this process easier?

What are some different ways to solve the problem that haven't been thought of yet?

What can I do to question or change the way things are now?

What are some ways I could use technology to make things better?

How can I turn this difficulty into a chance?

What would I do if I had an endless supply of money or time?

Remember that the key is to ask open-ended questions that make people think and allow for more than one answer. Let your mind wander, and your thoughts will flow easily. Even if you think your ideas are strange or won't work, write them down. Sometimes, the most creative ideas come from asking questions and looking for ways to do things that aren't clear. nformation that supports the assumption in a critical

So, if you want to come up with some fresh concepts, try posing some novel questions. Here are some general questions you can ask on a regular basis to make questioning a part of your everyday routine.

Why do I do things a certain way when it comes to my most important project?

Then you need to develop a more compelling response to this question and act on it. If you ask the question more than once and don't get a better answer, it's time to change your method or the work itself.

If you keep asking yourself that question and coming up empty, it may be time to rethink your strategy or maybe abandon the project altogether.

What else can I do to get my work done more quickly?

Your first inclination in response to this inquiry will likely be to fire up Google and write, "How to do ___________ (fill in the blank with your task) in half the time and cost?" Or ask if there is a way to hire someone else to do the work for a fraction of what my time would cost.

Or I could see if there's a way to outsource the task, since I'm sure someone else could do it for much less.

Who should I talk to or seek advice from to speed up my personal development?

This question should make you reach for a pen and paper right away and start writing down the names of people you know who you think can help you figure out better ways to do the work.

The moment you hear this question, you should grab a pen and paper and start writing down the names of the people you know who you believe can help you offer better ways of handling the work.

When is the best time to do something so that I get the most return on my time investment (ROTI)?

When should I do this or that to get the most return on my time investment (ROTI)?

You'll notice that there are times in your day when you have more energy to do hard work or when it's quieter and less distracting, and you should do your most focused work.

You'll find that there are optimal times during the day to get your most productive work done, such as when you feel most energised to tackle challenging tasks or when the office is the quietest and you're less likely to be interrupted.

You might feel more energised and motivated to start your most important job early in the morning when most people are still asleep at home. On the other hand, you might be a night owl who wants to keep going late into the night.

It's possible that you're a morning person who is at their most productive first thing in the morning when everyone else is still in bed, or that you're a night owl who thrives on working late into the night.

How can I improve the quality of my daily life, my relationships with other people, and my overall sense of well-being?

Seeking an answer to this question may cause you to consider other strategies for evoking these sentiments. You may spend the weekend researching conferences and activities that will broaden your perspective and expand your alternatives. You could try meditating more intensely to get the answers you're looking for. way and

Use a wide variety of interrogative prefixes, like

Why?

Where?

Whom?

When?

How?

Where?

Whether?

If

For your convenience, I have provided a collection of example questions. Now is the time to sit down with a pen and paper and ask yourself these questions about the things that are most important to you in life: your personal life, your career, your relationships, your family, your adventures, and your spirituality.

Don't stop jotting down random thoughts. You'll either learn what you need to know or generate new questions that require additional reading, interviews, or experiments.

A sincere effort like this is guaranteed to provide many ideas, some of which may turn out to be game-changing breakthroughs in your line of work.

However, the secret is to always be curious. Don't settle for things as they are or let life carry on as usual. The appropriate questions might help you come up with a wide variety of fresh concepts.

Share Your Ideas with People Who Aren't Specialists

There have been times when specialists advised against or even cancelled research efforts that ultimately turned out to be fruitful. Let's see Just a few instances:

One of the most well-known instances is the development of penicillin by Alexander Fleming. In 1928, Fleming discovered that Penicillium notatum mould had contaminated his bacterial culture plates, stunting the growth of his microorganisms. Fleming saw the value in his accidental discovery, but many medical professionals at the time were sceptical of its potential. It wasn't until Howard Florey and his colleagues refined and successfully mass-produced penicillin in the 1940s that the drug's potentially life-saving properties became widely known.

In the 1960s, Arno Penzias and Robert Wilson were using a sensitive microwave antenna at Bell Labs when they noticed a constant background noise in their observations; this noise would later be identified as the cosmic microwave background radiation (CMB). At first, they suspected that it was caused by a technical glitch or pigeon poop in their antenna. They consulted professionals, who advised them to clean the antenna and get rid of any interference. However, despite my best efforts, the noise remained. The discovery of cosmic microwave background radiation in the late 1970s provided substantial support for the Big Bang theory and resulted in the award of the 1978 Nobel Prize in Physics to the team.

What do these historical instances have in common? Experts' terrible predictions about the new ideas burst, and in the end, they proved to be a historic breakthrough.:

Ralph Waldo Emerson, an American essayist, philosopher, and poet who played a significant role in shaping American literature and thought during the mid-19th century, rightly said.

"The greatest glory in living lies not in never falling but in rising every time we fall."

The most important thing to remember is that you shouldn't consult experts when you need to come up with new and original concepts.

Professional advice and guidance are significant. But if people are encouraged to look for answers elsewhere, they may discover novel viewpoints, original concepts, and game-changing breakthroughs that traditional thinking has overlooked.

The following methods can be used to solicit and encourage perspectives from others who aren't experts in the field:

Take part in free-form conversations: It's beneficial to talk to people who have varying levels of knowledge and experience. Seek out the perspectives of those who aren't directly involved in your sector or industry.

Collaborate with diverse teams: Create groups that include people with a wide range of experiences, expertise, and perspectives. Gathering people from different backgrounds might help you gain access to new ideas and viewpoints.

Seek feedback from unrelated fields: Get opinions from people in completely different fields than your own and see what they think about your ideas and problems. People from different fields may have novel ideas and approaches that might spark creativity.

Engage with user communities: Participate in user communities If your project or study targets a particular demographic of end-users or customers, you should participate in their community. Pay attention to their comments, questions, and ideas.

Attend interdisciplinary conferences or events: Go to gatherings of specialists from various professions. Going to seminars or workshops on topics outside your field of expertise is a great way to learn about new concepts, network with people from different backgrounds, and broaden your perspective.

Embrace online platforms and communities: Participate actively in online communities by joining relevant online forums and social media groups and talking to people who share your interests or who work in related professions.

Encourage anonymous or confidential feedback: Promote feedback that is anonymous or confidential by making it possible for people to share their thoughts and ideas without worrying about repercussions.

Keep in mind that you shouldn't just ignore popular wisdom in favour of your own research and intuition. Seeking out the perspectives of those who aren't experts in the field might help you learn more, test your own beliefs, and find novel approaches to problems.

Tips for letting Procrastination Ferment Your Ideas

Procrastination can be used to come up with new ideas and be more creative. Here are a few ways to use putting things off to come up with ideas:

Know the Difference: Know that there is a difference between putting things off without getting anything done and putting things off on purpose. Unproductive procrastination means putting off chores and wasting time. On the other hand, purposeful incubation means setting aside time to think and let ideas develop.

Set Intentional Incubation Time: Set aside specific times in your plan for incubation. This can be a set amount of time every day or specific chunks of time spread out over the week when you give yourself permission to let your mind wander and try out new ideas.

Do Mindless Things: Doing things that don't require much thought can give your mind a break and help you come up with new ideas. You can take a break from focused work by going for a walk, doing light housework, or doing some light physical activity.

Capture thoughts and ideas: Keep a notebook or digital tool ready to write down any ideas or insights that come to you while you're putting things off. Taking a break from your job can help you think of new ideas or connections.

Find Ideas and Input: When you're putting things off, use the time to look for ideas in different places. Read books, papers, or blogs about things that interest you; talk to other people; or try out different kinds of media.

Accept Time Off: Give yourself time off without feeling bad about it. Rest and relaxation are important for recharging your creative energy and making you feel better.

Remember that putting things off can be good for coming up with ideas, but it's important to find a balance and not make it a habit to put off important chores.

Lin-Manuel Miranda, an American playwright, composer, and actor best known for his musicals "Hamilton" and "In the Heights," has discussed the importance of procrastination to his work. He says that he frequently lets his mind roam and ponders concepts without immediate pressure, which enables his brain to develop unexpected connections and produce novel ideas.

The great American science fiction writer Isaac Asimov said that delay played a part in his work. He said that he occasionally engaged in deliberate procrastination to enable his thoughts to meander and investigate novel possibilities. He thought he was more creative since he took his time thinking about things and drawing conclusions.seless.

It was the most significant evening of 1963 for Martin Luther King Jr., who would give the most significant speech of his life the following day.

He stayed up until 3 in the morning revising, cutting, and polishing his speech.

After that, he sat in the audience and continued to make notes and minor adjustments to his prepared statement. The moment finally came, and he stood up there with his speech notes in hand. But just a few minutes into the speech, he set aside his prepared message and said the four words that changed the course of history: "I have a dream."

These were unplanned additions to his speech. He delayed writing his speech until the eleventh hour so that he could give his ideas more time to percolate.

This is the crucial piece of information.

In terms of efficiency, procrastination is a sin, but when it comes to original thought, it can be a blessing. When used strategically it helps in creativity.

Mark Twain was an American author who believed that people who put things off often had better ideas. He was known for his famous books and for putting things off and working under a lot of stress. His quote, "If it's your job to eat a frog, do it first thing in the morning," suggests that putting things off can create a sense of urgency and help people think more clearly. Twain also often put off writing when he should have been doing it, creating a fresh, natural style that kept readers interested.

In his TED talk, Adam Grant explains why procrastinators often have better ideas. Some participants were invited to come up with fresh company concepts for the study. They were split in half. One set of people was tasked with starting work right away. The second group was given five to ten minutes to play a game before they were asked to come up with any concrete suggestions. The latter group was found to have a 16% higher rate of originality. Assumption challenging: Assumption challenging is the process of tantly ng

for what reason did this occur?

The game they played wasn't anything out of the ordinary. They were able to think of more imaginative solutions because they were instructed to work on a problem and then given the freedom to put off solving the issue; the procrastination allowed the task to remain in the back of their minds, where it may generate solutions. F

Research shows that people often have the best ideas when they are not trying to think of them. Diffuse and divergent thinking can help people think creatively and come up with new ideas. Unexpected moments can lead to great ideas and products, and a mix of focused work and time to rest and relax can help people be more creative. In the beginning of his work, Sorkin had the bad habit of putting off writing. He often didn't start working on his writing until the last minute, which put a lot of stress and pressure on him. But Sorkin's creativity seemed to flourish when he was under pressure to meet a timetable.

Sorkin wrote "A Few Good Men" in a short amount of time, even though he was stressed and short on time, and was able to finish the writing in that short amount of time.

The result was a highly popular and well-reviewed play that was put on Broadway and then turned into a hit movie.

All the cases above show that the idea of incubation works. You have already done the hard work of filling your conscious mind with a lot of knowledge, so your subconscious mind is constantly processing new information.

That's why it's best to work on multiple projects at once, as we talked about in our earlier point about how slow it is to do more than one thing at once.

Even though you are no longer working on the task, your mind is still working on it in the background. The more you want to figure out how to solve a problem, the more likely it is that your mind will come up with ideas. hat reason did this occur?

Follow the steps below to start incubation and keep track of the process well:

Describe the issue: Say what the problem or job is that you want to solve. For example, if you're making a new product, you should list the main benefits, the people you want to reach, and the results you want.

Focus on your work: Give yourself time to work on the problem. For example, if you are working on a marketing effort, you should spend a lot of time doing market research, analysing the strategies of your competitors, and coming up with creative ideas.

Step away on purpose: Once you've been working hard on something, choose to step away from the problem on purpose. Stop thinking about it and do something else for a while. Some examples are going for a walk-in nature, practising relaxation, or doing something you enjoy.

Create space in your mind: During the break, avoid thinking about the problem directly to create space in your mind. Let go of your worries and pressure about finding an answer right now. For example, if you're trying to come up with a business plan, don't think about your budget or what other people expect of you.

Believe in the process: Have faith that your mind can work on the problem without you being aware of it. Believe that new ideas and links will come to you on their own. For instance, if you're a writer who can't think of anything to write, trust that thoughts will come to you when you least expect them to.

Stay open and aware: During and after the incubation time, stay open to thoughts, insights, and connections that come to you out of the blue. For example, if you're making a website, you might get ideas by looking at buildings or art.

Keep a notebook or digital device: Keep a notebook or digital device close by to write down any ideas or insights that come to you during or after the incubation time. For example, if you're making a new recipe, try out different ingredients and ways of cooking based on what you learned in the incubation process.

What should you do right now?

When you face a problem, the first thing you should do is learn as much as you can about it. Read a lot of books.

Google or use ChatGPT to get all the information you can find and look for movies, blogs, and podcasts about the topic. When you've done enough study, your head will start to spin with all the information you've learned. This means that you have loaded your prefrontal cortex, which is the part of your brain that helps you learn new things.

Now, take a break from the problem for a day or two or work on something else. This will start the incubation process, and all the research you've done will start to be processed in your head. You might come up with a better answer than if you had forced your head to come up with one.

Stay calm and wait for your "Aha!" time to come. It will come at a time and place you don't expect it to, most of the time.

Take it easy Technique

The Take it easy Technique is a way to relax that is meant to help people slow down and feel less stressed. It's as easy as changing your attention and focusing it on certain things around you or inside your body. You can use the method anywhere and at any time when you want to relax and calm down.

Here's how to use the Take it easy Technique, step by step:

Find a good place to sit: Find a place where you can sit or lay down that is quiet and comfortable. It could be a chair, a couch, or even the floor, depending on what you find most comfortable.

Deep breathing: Take a few deep breaths in through your nose. As you breathe in, let your stomach expand. Then slowly let out your breath through your mouth, letting go of any worry or tension with each breath.

Scan your body: Close your eyes and think about your whole body, from your head to your toes. Notice any places where you feel tightness or pain. Pay attention to any tightness, pain, or other feelings you may have.

Relaxation timer: Imagine a countdown from ten to one. As you count down, picture each number. Imagine that your body is getting calmer and more at ease with each number. For instance, when you get to ten, picture your head and hair relaxing. As you count down from ten to nine, picture your neck and shoulders getting loose and relaxed.

Watch what's going on around you: Open your eyes and pay attention to what's around you. Look around and notice the colours, shapes, and textures of the things you see. Watch anything that moves or stays still around you.

Engage your senses: Focus on what you can hear, see, smell, taste, and touch to fully engage your senses. Notice the sounds around you, how the surface you're sitting or lying on feels, any smells in the air, and any tastes that are still in your mouth.

Grounding exercise: Do a grounding exercise to bring your mind back to the present moment. Pay attention to how your feet feel when they touch the ground. Feel the support under you and picture yourself as a part of the earth.

Affirmations: Say or think out loud positive words or ones that make you feel better. These can be simple sentences like "I'm calm and at ease" or "I'm in charge of my feelings" or any other words that make sense to you.

Stay in the moment: Finally, give yourself permission to stay in the present and enjoy the calm and ease you've built up. If your thoughts start to come up or your mind starts to wander, gently bring your attention back to your breath or the feelings in your body.

The Take it easy Technique is a flexible way to relax that you can change to fit your tastes and needs. It can be a short exercise if you only have a few minutes to spend or a longer one if you have more time. When you use this method on a regular basis, it can help you feel calmer, reduce stress, and improve your overall health.Th

Note that the sun's brightness obscures the stars, so they can't be seen during the day. Your original thoughts are, too, because the constant chatter in your head drowns them out.

Thoughts are already floating around out there. The channels in your head are like radio stations; you can only hear them when you tune in to the correct frequency. When you're calm and meditative, your mind can open up to new possibilities, and you can serve as a conduit for creative solutions to difficulties' Just Chill Technique is a way to relax that is meant to help

There are usually obvious solutions to our problems, but we don't take the time to calm our thoughts enough to notice them. attention and focusing it on certain things nd you or inside our

Let's take the example of Walt Disney. It is a synonym for invention and imagination. Walt Disney was one of the people who started The Walt Disney Company. He made his daydreams come true by making famous characters like Mickey Mouse and theme parks like Disneyland and Walt Disney World. His ideas changed the leisure business and made millions of people happy around the world.any

In another example Mark Zuckerberg one of the people who started Facebook, which has brought together billions of people all over the world. Zuckerberg had a dream that the internet would bring people together and make a global community. His big ideas made Facebook one of the most important and widely used tools, changing how people talk to each other and share information.

Calvert Impact Capital was formed by Wayne Silby, who later put "Chief Daydreamer" as his title on his business cards. He had a habit of using a warm water tank bath as a means of self-reflection and idea generation. He explains that he joined the tank because he needed to figure out how to compete with banks during a time when the government was modifying regulations governing money market deposits. While I was floating in the tank, I decided to join them. In the end, we came up with a $800 million plan. In many cases, the answers to our issues are already within us; we just need to sit still long enough to hear them.

Let's understand the different types of Brainwaves.

Beta waves (12–30 Hz) are related to awake, alert states of mind, such as when we are working or paying attention to anything outside ourselves. One's ability to think critically, make decisions, and solve problems proactively all depend on these abilities.

Alpha Waves (8–12 Hz): We produce alpha waves when our minds are at rest but alert, such as in meditation or mild daydreaming. They're linked to a stress-free state of mind, greater inventiveness, and better comprehension.

Getting into an alpha brainwave state can be achieved through various relaxation techniques and practises. Here's a roadmap that can help you reach an alpha brainwave state:

Find a quiet and comfortable space: Start by finding a quiet environment where you can relax without distractions. It could be a peaceful room or a serene outdoor setting.

Adopt a relaxed posture: Sit or lie down in a comfortable position. Make sure your body is supported and you can fully relax without straining.

Deep breathing: Begin by taking slow, deep breaths in through your nose, allowing your abdomen to expand. Then exhale slowly through your mouth, releasing any tension with each breath. Focus on the sensation of your breath as it enters and leaves your body.

Progressive muscle relaxation: To relax your body further, engage in progressive muscle relaxation. Start by tensing and then releasing each muscle group in your body, starting from your toes and working your way up to your head. Pay attention to the feeling of relaxation as you release the tension in each muscle group.

Visualise calming imagery: Close your eyes and visualise a peaceful and serene scene. It could be a tranquil beach, a peaceful garden, or any other calming environment that brings you a sense of relaxation. Engage your senses in this visualisation, imagining the sights, sounds, and even smells associated with that place.

Focus on your breath or a repetitive sound: Direct your attention to your breath or a repetitive sound, such as a soothing mantra or the sound of gentle music. Use this as an anchor to bring your focus back whenever your mind starts to wander.

Practise mindfulness or meditation: Engage in mindfulness or meditation techniques to cultivate a state of present-moment awareness. Allow your thoughts to come and go without judgement, gently redirecting your focus to your breath or chosen focal point whenever you become aware of mental distractions.

Practise regularly: Consistency is key when training your brain to enter an alpha brainwave state. Set aside dedicated time for relaxation and practise the techniques regularly to train your mind to shift into a relaxed and calm state.

Through deep breathing and meditation, you can transform into the conduit through which any difficulty dissolves on its own. The method results in slower, more in-depth brain waves called alpha. If you can achieve an alpha state transition in your brainwaves, you'll be able to generate and attract solutions because the alpha waves will calm your mind and allow you to notice them.me when you want to relax and calm down.

Chapter 6 Key Takeaways

Verify all defaults and assumptions. Never take something at face value; always ask why. You can't compel your brain to consider different options until you first question the status quo or default assumption.

There is power in questions. You get out of life what you put into it, so ask yourself good questions. Albert Einstein, Isaac Newton, and Elon Musk are just a few examples of innovators who are known for their penchant for asking provocative questions. Curiosity is fed and new ideas are sparked when you actively seek answers to your inquiries. If you want to be more creative when you need it, just ask yourself, "What, Why, When, Where, and How?" in response to any problem.

Share your ideas with people who aren't experts. Experts may know a lot about one specific area, but they often know relatively little about other, more general topics. British author Arthur C. Clarke summed up this idea thus: "If an elderly but distinguished scientist says that something is possible, he is almost certainly right; but if he says that it is impossible, he is very probably wrong." When you're trying to come up with new ideas, it's a good idea to hear what regular people think.

Procrastination Ferment Your Ideas. Though it's a productivity sin, procrastination can be a creative blessing. If artists procrastinate long enough, new connections can form between their disparate ideas.

Take it easy Technique. This is more of a passive technique to generate innovative ideas. You transition yourself from distractive and noisy beta brainwaves to relaxing alpha brainwaves. And this lets your mind get into more of an imaginative and daydreaming state, where you can invite more ideas. How to use the Just Chill Technique, step by step:

Conclusion

****

"Imagination is the fuel of innovation. It is the spark that ignites the fire of creativity, propelling us to explore uncharted territories and revolutionize the world around us."

- Oprah Winfrey

We have now reached the end of the book.

You now have all the knowledge you need to fully comprehend the process of creative problem-solving. You have a wide toolkit of creative thinking strategies at your disposal.

While reading this book, you should be able to put the methods it describes into practise. I trust you set aside some time to practise the exercises along the way, and if yes, then you've already noticed an improvement in your ability for creative thinking.

But I get that before attempting to execute that, some individuals want to read the whole book to get a firm grasp on the topic. If that describes you, have no fear; you may begin doing the exercises again and witness the results for yourself right away.

Okay, I'll be honest. Though I write my books to help others (that's you!), I always have some underlying reason in mind, like the possibility that I might learn something useful during my study that I could put to use in my own life.

To put into practise what we have read and to enrich our experience of life via the exploration of many methods of creative thinking, I thus encourage you to join me on this journey.

I've included a summary of each chapter's key points at the end of each chapter, so you can gain an overview with no effort.

We all know that practise makes perfect. Let's keep feeding our brains useful information on a regular basis so that we can cultivate an original outlook and experience success, happiness, and fulfilment in all areas of life.

I hope you find tremendous success in all you do by thinking creatively and acting on those thoughts.

Cheersings" or any other word

s://startuptalky.com/taco-bell-marketing-gy/
tps://www.fond.co/blog/levers-onboarding-startup-success/

Could I possibly ask a favour of you?

I'd like to start off by saying how much I appreciate you picking up this book and giving it a read. I appreciate that you picked my book instead of someone else's.

Ideally, you were able to take away a few nuggets of wisdom that will make a difference in your day-to-day operations.

Please give me another 30 seconds of your time.

Please consider writing a review of the book and sending it my way. While reviews may not have much of an impact on best-selling authors, they are incredibly helpful to unknown authors like me. They help me attract more readers by convincing more people to give my work a try.

To put it frankly, reviews are a writer's bread and butter.

Please leave a review; it will take less than a minute of your time but will greatly assist me in reaching more people.

Your belief in what I do is greatly appreciated. That evaluation would be very appreciated. you.

Stay in the moment: Finally, give yourself permission to stay in the present and enjoy the calm anuilt up. If your thoughts start to come up or your mind starts to wander, gently bring your attention back to your breath or the feelings in your body.

The Just Chill Technique is a flexible way to relax that you can change to fit your tastes and needs. It can be a short exercise if you only have a few minutes to spend or a longer one if you have more time. When you use this method on a regular basis, it can help you feel calmer, reduce stress, and improve your overall health.

solutions because they were instructed to work on a problem and then given the freedom to put off solving the issue; the procrastination allowed the task to remain in the back of their minds, where it may

Full book summary solute

is built and looks

Chapter 1 Introduction: Key Takeaways

If you think creatively, you can find more solutions to any problem, even if there only appear to be a few.

Anyone, whether an individual or a large corporation, can improve upon their current operations and point of view by taking a fresh look at the situation. The personal and organisational examples show how thinking creatively can lead to novel insights and fresh ways of perceiving the world.

Furthermore, creative problem solving is not restricted to a select group of artistically endowed people or reality-bending, world-changing business leaders. If one believes they can learn how to think creatively and is ready to put in the time and effort to do so, they will enhance their creative thinking abilities and discover unexpectedly new and unpredictable ways of addressing problems.

Every growth-oriented person **who wants to discover and direct their life in ways they couldn't have imagined before** will find useful information and guidance in this book.

at other points of view or **Chapter 2: Key Takeaways**

For much of human history, up until the middle of the twentieth century, **the conventional wisdom held that the left hemisphere of the brain is the more evolved and useful of the two**, while the right hemisphere is home to hopelessly unrealistic ideas that have no place in the real world.

The work of Nobel laureate and neurologist Robert Sperry has shown **how the right hemisphere of the brain is crucial for seeing the big picture** and understanding the world around us. Later, Betty Edwards's book "Drawing from the Right Side of the Brain" and the development of fMRI in neuroscience provided unmistakable confirmation of the symmetry between the two hemispheres.

The left side of the brain controls the right side of the body, and the right side of the brain controls the left side of the body. The left is sequential, and the right is simultaneous. The left side of the brain looks at the words, while the right side looks at the bigger picture. The left brain looks at things in a logical way, while the right brain puts things together.

The way you think is like a box. Both the number of objects and the kinds of items that can be stored in a given box are limited. Similarly, we have a habit of thinking in a certain way on a consistent basis. This way of thinking is typically restricted and governed by the kinds of ideas that are instilled in us from early childhood all the way through adulthood. **The result is that we can only think in the limited ways that our conditioning has taught us.**

The Quadrant challenge and 9-dot exercise are useful tool for evaluating your thought process, whether you tend to stick to tried-and-true methods or seek novel approaches when faced with a challenge. The only way to think creatively and generate original ideas is to leave the safety of the familiar and explore the infinite possibilities beyond.

Chapter 3: Key Takeaways

The first step is to have faith. If you don't have faith in yourself and your abilities, you won't act in ways that reflect those beliefs. No faith, no hope, no change. Strong conviction >> huge actions >> greater outcomes >> even stronger convictions is the formula.

Fear, uncertainty, and doubt (FUDs) are the three main obstacles to creating a strong belief, and as long as they are in your thoughts, you won't believe that you can think creatively and provide creative responses.

You need to strengthen not one but two key beliefs. (1) that you can carry out your assigned duties; (2) that you possess the same inherent skills as anyone else.

The tick-tock method can help you build strong convictions. Create a "tick" column for each false belief and a "tock" column for each objective argument that refutes it.

If you want to change your worldview, **using self-affirmations in the form of "commitment"** will get you there faster.

Spend as little time as possible with negative people and maximise your time with those who inspire confidence in you.

Focusing on your accomplishments rather than your setbacks will help you move forward positively.

Chapter 4: Key Takeaways

Science has shown that playing an instrument can help you become more creative. To generate more ideas on autopilot, it may be most helpful to establish a small number of routines.

Memory and creativity enhancing BDNF are enhanced by physical activity. Increase your BDNF levels by exercising vigorously.

The release of dopamine after a shower has been scientifically confirmed. Dopamine levels correlate with the likelihood of having novel thoughts. Thus, you should bathe more frequently.

Practise a form of meditation based on "open monitoring." You'll be able to observe more, including the inner workings of your body and organs, the sights, sounds, and smells of your surroundings, and your own mental processes. Your ability to think in novel ways will increase as you increase your capacity for observation.

Disconnect from social media and instead focus your attention on something you truly value.As

You need to broaden your perspective on life in general and embrace the specific challenge of coming up with ideas. Having more life experiences increases neuroplasticity, which in turn provides more opportunities for your brain to be creative.

As your mind wants to be sure of the **advantages of being creative**, it will develop more ideas in response to a specific and significant challenge than to merely sit and wait for ideas.

nd wants to be sure of advantages of being creative, it will develop more ideas in response to a specific e to **Chapter 5: Key Takeaways** me

Embrace boredom to foster idea generation. When you're bored, you're not driven by your constant desires and distractions. You will experience boredom if you do nothing. The DMN, or imagining network, of your brain is triggered when you allow yourself to become bored.

Nourish your mind extensively before you try to generate completely new ideas. "The function of education is to teach one to think intensively and critically. Intelligence plus character—that is the goal of true education." Martin Luther King Jr. Reading widely, particularly biographies and works on topics outside of one's own expertise, might help cultivate an environment in which new ideas can flourish.

Combining Ideas to Create Novel Concepts. There is a lack of original thought, and most innovations merely improve upon or combine past developments. Now that you've stuffed your brain with ideas, it's time to start putting them to use. Using a technique like mind mapping to get your scattered thoughts down on paper can help you better combine them.

Use Brainstorming Method to Quickly Generate Many Ideas. It fosters an atmosphere where people feel comfortable expressing their ideas without worrying about being criticised or dismissed. That independence allows for the discovery of novel approaches that would not have been possible with more conventional ways of thinking.

Use the SCAMPER method. Using this strategy, you'll have access to seven distinct ways of inquiring into your own character. To come up with new ideas, you can use the letters in the acronym SCAMPER to come up with questions to ask.

The Advantages of Creative Multitasking. Instead of constantly switching between different jobs, you should immerse yourself in multiple projects at once. This allows you to take a step back from the task at hand, clearing your head so that you can come up with more refined solutions. Working on many tasks together also allows you to accomplish more.

Establish a daily idea limit. You should set a goal to come up with at least five new ideas for your tasks or problems every day. Having good ideas requires daily exercise. The higher the quantity of ideas from which to choose, the higher the quality of the ideas you'll ultimately choose.

a?ro drain. The same thing h**Chapter 6: Key Takeaways**

Verify all defaults and assumptions. Never take something at face value; always ask why. You can't compel your brain to consider different options until you first question the status quo or default assumption.

There is power in questions. You get out of life what you put into it, so ask yourself good questions. Albert Einstein, Isaac Newton, and Elon Musk are just a few examples of innovators who are known for their penchant for asking provocative questions. Curiosity is fed and new ideas are sparked when you actively seek answers to your inquiries. If you want to be more creative when you need it, just ask yourself, "What, Why, When, Where, and How?" in response to any problem.

Share your ideas with people who aren't experts. Experts may know a lot about one specific area, but they often know relatively little about other, more general topics. British author Arthur C. Clarke summed up this idea thus: "If an elderly but distinguished scientist says that something is possible, he is almost certainly right; but if he says that it is impossible, he is very probably wrong." When you're trying to come up with new ideas, it's a good idea to hear what regular people think.

Procrastination Ferment Your ideas. Though it's a productivity sin, procrastination can be a creative blessing. If artists procrastinate long enough, new connections can form between their disparate ideas.

Take it easy Technique. This is more of a passive technique to generate innovative ideas. You transition yourself from distractive and noisy beta brainwaves to relaxing alpha brainwaves. And this lets your mind get into more of an imaginative and daydreaming state, where you can invite more ideas. How to use the Just Chill Ten y shift it between

Could you please leave a review on the book

One last time!

Please consider writing a review of the book and sending it my way. While reviews may not have much of an impact on best-selling authors, those like me who are just starting out really appreciate them.

They aid in expanding my reader base by sparking the interest of potential buyers.

To put it frankly, reviews are a writer's bread and butter.

Please leave a review; it will take less than a minute of your time but will greatly assist me in reaching more people.

I appreciate your interest in my work and look forward to reading your book review.t

https://startuptalky.com/taco-bell-marketing-strategy/

https://www.fond.co/blog/levers-onboarding-startup-success/

https://www.theguardian.com/sport/2020/may/27/charleston-riverdogs-nobody-night-promotion-baseball-no-fans#:~:text=This%20was%20%E2%80%9CNobody%20Night%E2%80%9D[1].

https://www.researchgate.net/publication/8084569_A_Meta-Analysis_of_Personality_in_Scientific_and_Artistic_Creat

https://www.ncbi.nlm.nih.gov/pmc/articles/PMC3897366/

https://gwern.net/doc/psychology/1998-feist.pdf

https://www.industryleadersmagazine.com/a-mcdonalds-run-by-robots-the-start-of-an-automated-future/#:~:text=McDonalds%20run%20by%20robots%3A%20%20E2%80%9C[2]

https://www.ncbi.nlm.nih.gov/pmc/articles/PMC3772595/

---

1.   https://www.theguardian.com/sport/2020/may/27/charleston-riverdogs-nobody-night-promotion-baseball-no-fans#_853ae90f0351324bd73ea615e6487517__4c761f170e016836ff84498202b99827__853ae90f0351324bd73ea615e6487517_text_43ec3e5dee6e706af7766fffea512721_This_0bcef9c45bd8a48eda1b26eb0c61c869_20was_0bcef9c45bd8a48eda1b26eb0c61c869_20_0bcef9c45bd8a48eda1b26eb0c61c869_E2_0bcef9c45bd8a48eda1b26eb0c61c869_80_0bcef9c45bd8a48eda1b26eb0c61c869_9CNobody_0bcef9c45bd8a48eda1b26eb0c61c869_20Night_0bcef9c45bd8a48eda1b26eb0c61c869_E2_0bcef9c45bd8a48eda1b26eb0c61c869_80_0bcef9c45bd8a48eda1b26eb0c61c869_9D_0bcef9c45bd8a48eda1b26eb0c61c869_2C_c0cb5f0fcf239ab3d9c1fcd31fff1efc_through_0bcef9c45bd8a48eda1b26eb0c61c869_20gaps_0bcef9c45bd8a48eda1b26eb0c61c869_20in_0bcef9c45bd8a48eda1b26eb0c61c869_20the_0bcef9c45bd8a48eda1b26eb0c61c869_20gates

2.   https://www.industryleadersmagazine.com/a-mcdonalds-run-by-robots-the-start-of-an-automated-future/%23:~:text=McDonalds%20run%20by%20robots%3A%20%20E2%80%9CFast%E2%80%9D%20Food%20With%20a%20Twist&text=The%20restaurant's%20app%20updates%2C%20food,the%20go%20or%20at%20home.

https://news.stanford.edu/2014/04/24/walking-vs-sitting-042414/

https://www.ncbi.nlm.nih.gov/pmc/articles/PMC3887545/

https://www.frontiersin.org/articles/10.3389/fpsyg.2012.00116/full

https://www.psychologicalscience.org/news/minds-business/observation-skills-may-be-key-ingredient-to-creativity.html#.WUPjYxPyvdQ[3]

http://contemplative-studies.org/wp/index.php/2015/07/25/beginning-meditation-getting-started-4-open-monitoring-meditation/https://www.npr.org/2013/05/10/182861382/the-myth-of-multitasking[4]

outcomes or situations that counter or question the assumption. It

---

3.   https://www.psychologicalscience.org/news/minds-business/observation-skills-may-be-key-ingredient-to-creativity.html%23.WUPjYxPyvdQ

4.   http://contemplative-studies.org/wp/index.php/2015/07/25/beginning-meditation-getting-started-4-open-monitoring-meditation/https:/www.npr.org/2013/05/10/182861382/the-myth-of-multitasking